THE AUTOBIOGRAPHY OF AN EX-GRENADIER GUARDSMAN

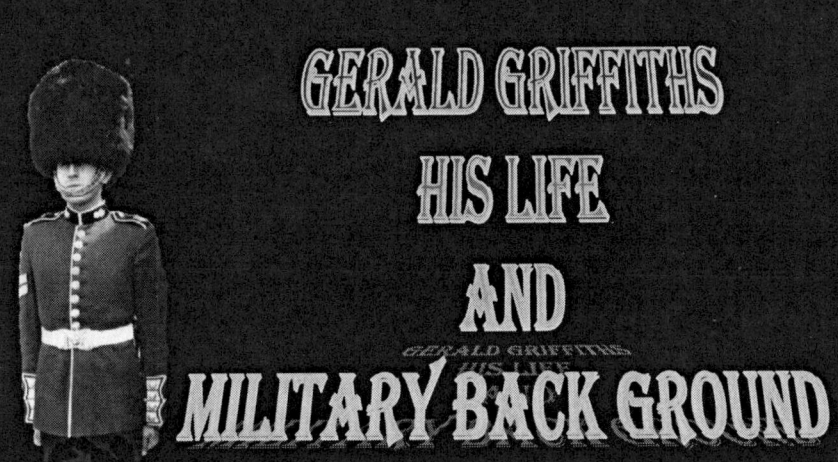

GERALD GRIFFITHS
HIS LIFE
AND
MILITARY BACK GROUND

THE GRENADIER GUARDS

This book is in memory of my Mum & Dad and past Family Members

I have written this book as I wanted to portray my exciting life during my Military Career, of the wonderful experience I had in the Grenadier Guards. I also wanted to point out the love and affection we all shared in a large family life, which started way back before the 2nd World War, The wonderful qualities of my Mother and Father, brothers and sisters, and the I love I have for them, plus those no longer with us, I miss them dreadfully. I wanted to be able to give my own Son and Grandchildren a keepsake they would be able to cherish for years to come, and hopefully show their children, and their childrens, children, the life of their Great Great Grandparents.

Gerald Glyn and June Montrose Griffiths.

23862933 L/Cpl Gerald Glyn Griffths

L/Cpl Griffiths 2nd Battalion Grenadier Guards 1961-1970. With three years on reserve.

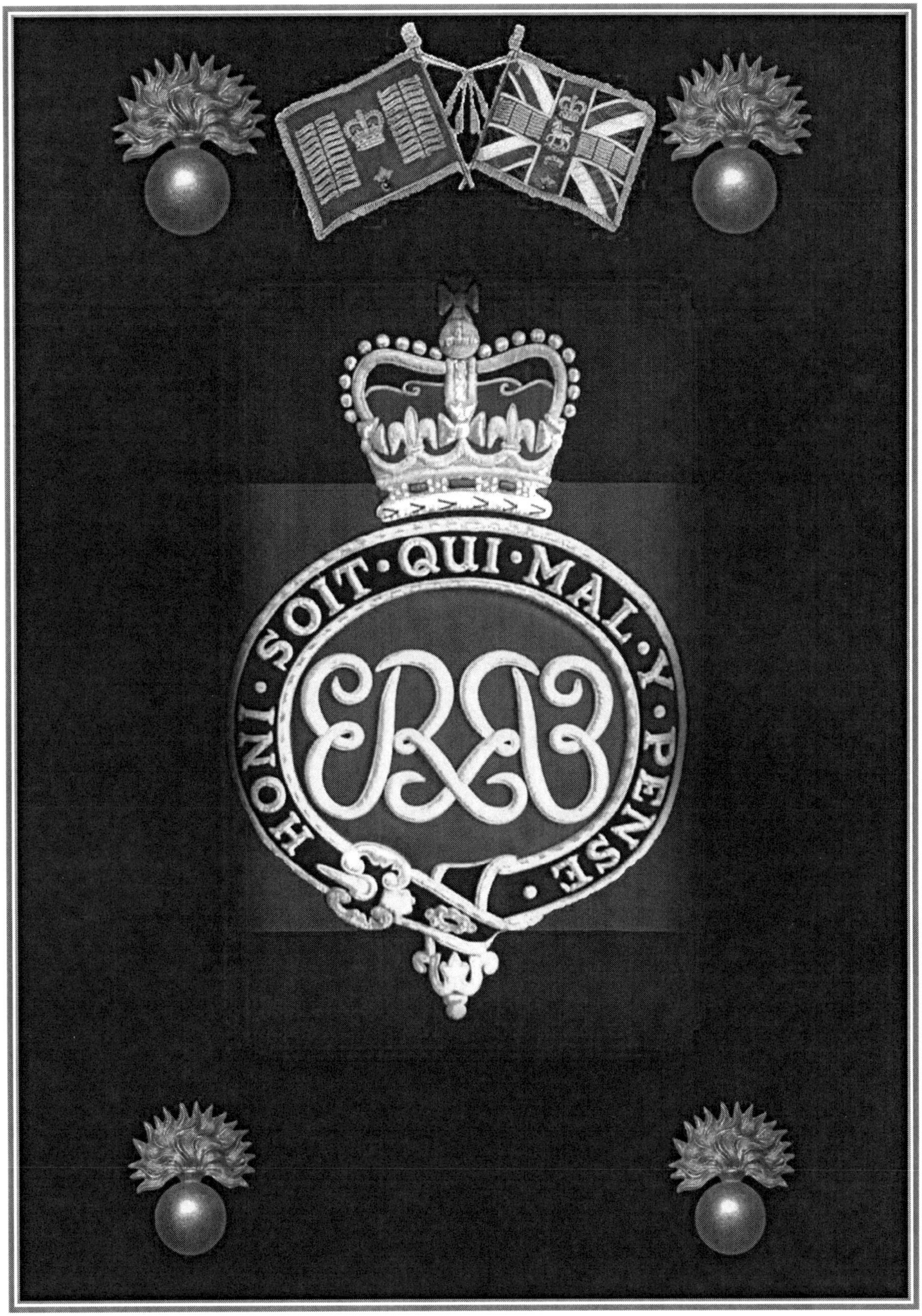
HONI · SOIT · QUI · MAL · Y · PENSE ·

Gerald Glyn Griffiths the author,
with his wife 'June Griffiths', 2010.

Dedications;

This book is dedicated with love, to my son, Graham John Griffiths and Granddaughter, Larrisa Fay Griffiths and Grandson, Brandon John Griffiths. To my Mum and Dad and all my Brothers and Sisters: Graham, David, Christopher, Sheila, Peter, Mary, Andrew and Angela, plus a very big thanks to all those who helped in contributing to my book, which I hope will be of immense pleasure to retain as a keepsake for generations to come.

Photo by Gareth Hughes.

The author Gerald Glyn Griffiths.

Ex-Grenadier Guard and

6th Dan Black-Belt in Karate, and a Master in Tai-Chi.

**Most of the photo's belong
To the Griffiths's Family and are copyright to them**

**The complete Graphical designs
of all the pages,and typing
by Gerald Glyn Griffiths.
Proofreading By Richard Lee Nettleton.**

AuthorHouse™
1663 Liberty Drive
Bloomington, IN 47403
www.authorhouse.com
Phone: 1-800-839-8640

© *2012 Gerald Griffiths. All rights reserved.*

No part of this book may be reproduced, stored in a retrieval system, or transmitted by any means without the written permission of the author.

Published by AuthorHouse 12/07/2012

ISBN: 978-1-4772-4721-1 (sc)
ISBN: 978-1-4772-4722-8 (ebk)

Any people depicted in stock imagery provided by Thinkstock are models, and such images are being used for illustrative purposes only.

Certain stock imagery © Thinkstock.

This book is printed on acid-free paper.
Because of the dynamic nature of the Internet, any web addresses or links contained in this book may have changed since publication and may no longer be valid. The views expressed in this work are solely those of the author and do not necessarily reflect the views of the publisher, and the publisher hereby disclaims any responsibility for them.

Acknowledgements and Thanks.

Mr. Colin Knight: I would to thank and acknowledge his outstanding work and the people he has helped. Everything he does is a tribute to him the Gloucestershire Branch, of the Grenadier Guards Association. I would also like to thank you Colin, for your kindness in helping June and I within the Grenadier Guards Association. Your dedication and hard work for the Association should be acknowledged far more than I can put here. 'Thank you Colin'.

Mr. Gareth Hughes: I would like to thank and acknowledge Gareth Hughes for giving me the inspiration to place the writings from my journal into book form. I would also like to thank him for inviting June and myself to his office at Cardiff University, and the great photographs he took during a photo shoot for my book. I would also like to thank him for the wonderful framed photo of June and myself. Thank you Gareth.

Mr. Robert Huntley: I would like to thank and acknowledge, Robert Huntley's outstanding achievements in grades and his ability in the Martial Arts, and for all the years of training and comradeship we have had together. Thank you Bob.

Mr. Richard Nettleton: I would like to thank and acknowledge Richard for his help and information on Photos and events which occurred, plus the considerable amount of proofreading he has helped me with, for without his help I do not know what I would have done. 'Thank you Richard'.

Thanks to Mrs. Jill Shelly and Mrs. Natalie Amy Paternoster and Mr. David Higgs: For allowing their photos to be published in my work.

Mr. Steve Walker: I would like to thank and acknowledge Steve for his kindness Steve is a person who would go out of his way to help a friend in need at any time of the day, or night, a very true friend. I would also like to acknowledge his dedication to practice, and his contribution to the administration of Shoto's-Traditional-Karate-Kai. Thank you Steve.

Mr. Phillip Knickenberg: Hi'ya Mate! It goes without saying to thank you for all your help with mechanics and motors. Without your help, 'Moggy' Morris Minor may not be on the road today, and would probably be in that great scrapheap in the sky. I would like to acknowledge all your dedication of our Martial Arts, and your work as Club Treasurer for Shoto's-Traditional-Karate-Kai. Thank you Phil.

Mrs. June Montrose Griffiths: Well what can I say? She is my wife! Thanks for putting up with me all these years, it goes without saying we love each other very much and hopes to have another 45 years together. Love you June.

Mr. Graham John Griffiths: I love you Son, 'you know that!' I would like to acknowledge the hardships you have gone through, and to tell you from Mum and myself, we love you very much, and think of you each day. Things are beginning to look good for the future, and we pray that a new love will be of great help to you within your life. We would like to thank you for helping Terese, bring into the world two beautiful Grandchildren, Larrisa and Brandon.

Mrs. Terese Fay, our Grandchildren's Mum: I would like to thank you for the beautiful Grandchildren, Larrisa and Brandon, and hope you have found happiness in your new family life. Good luck for the future.

Larrisa and Brandon: Mama and I love you both and miss you a lot. What can I say here? Well, I think Chapters 18 and 19 say it all, and it came from the bottom of our hearts to say these things. Thank you, we Love you so much, from Mama and Granddad.

Forword
By
Richard Lee Nettleton.

I was delighted when asked to write a forward for Gerald's forthcoming book.

I had known Gerald since our early days with the 2nd Battalion Grenadier Guards, from the mid 1960's onwards, but had lost touch with him over the years until recently.

Gerald was different from most Guardsmen, as he served with members of the Corps of Drums, in both his reconnaissance days, as well as his time with the assault Pioneers in Germany, and became accepted by them as one of their own.

I was a member of that same Corps of Drums, but had returned to the Guards Depot Pirbright by the time he joined the Assault Pioneers, so missed that part of his life, but do remember his excitement in barracks on the birth of his son!

It is said books are the window into the soul. In this book, you are able to glimpse many nostalgic moments from his early life, up until the present day. But, the one overriding factor, which has to be said, is his love and respect for his parents, family and friends, and his pride at having served in one of the Country's Elite Regiments, which shines through on each and every one of these pages. I found this a fascinating and exciting pictorial view into his life, and hope those reading this book will be able to do so as well.

Richard Lee Nettleton. 2011.

A brief record of Richard's service: His army number is: 23862965 and joined the Junior Guardsman's Company on 9th September 1961 aged 15, completed two Continental tours with them 1963 - 1964. Joined the 2nd Bn in Windsor in 1964, Germany 1966, back to the Guards Depot Corps of Drums in 1967, rejoined Battalion at Chelsea in 1969, Ireland 1969 - 1970, British Honduras 1972 and discharged in 1973. On noticing Richard's Army number it is so close to mine, which is 23862933.

Grenadier Guards Association,

Gloucestershire Branch.

Some very kind words written for me by Mr. Colin Knight, whom I have the deepest respect for, and is the Gloucestershire Branch Secretary of the Grenadier Guards Association.

Mr. Colin Knight.

Well, what can one say about Gerald Griffiths? Usually autobiographies are written by the rich and famous, or those who have held high office of some sort.

However, along comes Gerald and writes a detailed account of his life from his earliest memories, right up to the present day.

Having joined the Grenadier Guards, where 'Once a Grenadier always a Grenadier' is their motto, he has also joined an extended family, which will remain with him for the rest of his life.

He is, like most men who served in the Grenadier Guards, proud of his time with the Regiment, and rightly so. In this book, Gerald has recounted many interesting occasions and events during his life, all of which are meticulously recorded.

With regards to his Martial Arts. How many of us would have the dedication to attain the heights he has achieved? And although he cannot by any stretch of the imagination now be considered a young man, still practices these skills on a regular basis. Tell us the secret of your eternal youth Gerald; we would all like to know how you've achieved this.

Gerald and June have taken a big step by immigrating to Australia, and wish them well in their new environment. Now many miles away from his former home, Gerald still takes an interest in branch affairs and communicates with me as his Branch Secretary on a regular basis. However, I refuse to accept his excuse he's too far away to attend these meetings!

I understand he has already been on Australian Radio and Television, talking about the Grenadier Guards and his views on the Royal Wedding.

Watch this space I say, to see what else he gets involved in downunder.

From Colin Knight.

The Content 0f

The Autobiography of an ex Grenadier Guard

and

Martial Arts Instructor.

Chapters One to Twenty Four.

(1) The sadness at the loss of Mum and my younger sister. — Page (13).

(2) My Mum and Dad's life of how they met and the hardships of the War years. — Page (31).

(3) Gerald Glyn Griffiths Autobiography, his life and growing up. — Page (46).

(4) My life in the Grenadier Guards. — Page (79).

(5) Grenadiers in British Guyana as it was called then, and Guyana history. — Page (107).

(6) Back in Great Britain. Para course and King Hussein of Jordan, and Junior Guards Company. — Page (119).

(7) From Caterham we moved to Windsor and Ceremonial Duties. Bank of England and the 'Last Post'. — Page (134).

(8) More about Windsor Castle, This is where I met and fell in love and Married June. — Page (138).

(9) We moved to Germany in Wuppertal, we had a lovely baby son and named him Graham John. — Page (157)

(10) Gerald in Recognisance Platoon. And Pioneer Shop and becoming a None Commissioned Officer — Page (174)

(11) Back to London Ceremonial Duties at Chelsea Barracks. Lord Alexander of Tunis, and the Ceremony of the Keys Tower of London. — Page (180)

(12) The Presentation of the New Colours to the 2nd Gren Gds 1969, and deployment to Ireland, 1969. — Page (184)

(13) This is where I got demobbed, as the battalion was posted to Ireland — Page (186).

(14) I lost my Dad and sister Mary. Dedication for Mary. — Page (188).

(15) Peter came home from Australia to be with Mary. — Page (197)

(16) Back to the Rea Bridge Jet Harris party, and a trip to America, and wonderful times with Margret and Norman. — Page (202)

(17) Graham growing to be a fine young man & his life and Marriage to Terese Fay and birth of his children. — Page (127).

(18) The birth of Larrisa and Brandon. — Page (230)

(19) It's four in the morning, Larrisa and Brandon Growing up. Larrisa Growing to be a beautiful young Lady. — Page (241)

(20) Dedication to Andrew Bryant Griffiths. — Page (253)

(21) Grenadier Guards invitations to Buckingham Palace & Association Dinners & Dances. — Page (257)

(22) The Presentation of the 1st Battalion Grenadier Guards Colours at Buckingham Palace 2010 — Page (279)

(23) Our emigration to OZ, and Family photo's — Page (302)

(24) Bibliography & Index. — Page (314)

Chapter (1)

Gerald Griffiths

The Autobiography of his life,

Military back ground and Martial Arts history.

'Mine honour is my life, both grew as one.
Take honour from me, and my life is done. 'William Shakespeare.'

2009; Well, this is the year I decided to put all my scribbling and notes into print and start this book dedicated to my Son Graham, my grandchildren Brandon and Larrisa of which I am very proud, also to my Mother and Father and all my Brothers and Sisters. I hope you will not have found my writings to discursive, and that I have been able to hold your interest throughout.

I am starting this on a sad note as I want to get it out of the way. It is still early days as to what happened during this year, then I can concentrate on good memories.

This has been the saddest year of my life as I lost my dear Mum, as well as a sister during this year.
Dearest Mum died on the 4th May 2009 at 1-30pm at a care home at the old Vicarage in Frampton on Seven, Gloucestershire. She had nearly all her children around her when she peacefully slipped away in her sleep. She had a good innings, and lived to be a nice old age.

She was a very grand lady and was loved and liked by many people. Her house was an ever open door to whoever wanted to chat. She was forever cooking, and everyone who called received a piece of her apple tart, or cakes with their tea.
Oh! And her Curries were out of this world! She was doing these things right up until a few years before she died.
This same year my dear sister Angela, who came home from Australia to be with Mum, spending three months here before Mum died. After Mums death she went back to Australia on the 5th May 2009. We took her to the Airport ourselves, back to her babies as she would call her two grown up children, Alison and Paul and of course her Grandchildren Morgan, Will, and Hollie.

That following month she died herself, which was even more tragic as she had a wonderful man in her life, Carlwyn Saunders (Taff) and she had died on her Birthday.

Mum. Gran Griffiths, as everybody who knew her would call her Gran. This is Mum how everybody will remember her, old at ninety five, but sharp as a button.

She was so well liked: Her house was an ever open door.

I love you Mum, 'God bless'.

SPECIAL 'MUM' WHO HAS A WELCOME FOR EVERYONE

THE GAZETTE, FRIDAY, OCTOBER 2, 1987

"Mum" Griffiths, always busy. (87/1337)

A warm welcome, friendly smiles, offers of tea, coffee and huge slices of delicious home-made fruit cake and I had no need to ask the origin of 'Mum Griffiths' name!

Sitting in her small sitting room, sun streaming in the window, you could not do anything but relax and warm towards this mother of nine whose patience and generosity seem inexhaustible.

"The door is always open," said her third son Christopher. "There is always a cup of tea and something to eat for anyone who needs it."

And this is on top of bringing up nine children of her own!

The name 'Mum Griffiths', Gran or just plain Mum are used by all who know her as a tribute to her unconditional hospitality. "She was always

By ANNE MARSHALL

ready to help anyone — even if she didn't have a penny in her purse she would find something to give."

From family to friends, delivery men, road workers and bedraggled campers 'Mum Griffiths' would open her front door and welcome them in as part of her ever growing family.

"She is just never on her own and wherever she goes she makes more friends," explained Mary, her third youngest daughter as she told the story of the German campers her mother had taken in, how they kept in contact and even paid for their 'Mum' to visit them in Germany.

BATTLED

Looking back over the 73 years of her life, 'Mum Griffiths' shies away from presenting herself as the popular and well-loved person she is, but her children are not so reticent in describing the giving even when supplies appeared to have run dry.

She and her husband brought up their nine children — Graham, David, Christopher, Sheila, Gerald, Peter, Mary, Andrew and Angela during and after the war years, battling against bankruptcy, imminent homelessness and a subsiding house.

All the children helped around the home, cleaning, washing, running chores. "We used to have to walk five miles across Bristol to see my husband," Mum Griffiths remembered, "I had two in the pram and five following behind me when we went to the zoo."

It was at Bristol Zoo that the children used to wander round asking people for their empty pop bottles, gather them up, collect the threepenny refund and give the money to Mum to help with the housekeeping.

From Bristol the family moved to Slimbridge where Mum looked after the church and church hall and it was here that her motherhood extended to look after three of her grandchildren (her own youngest were still at home as well).

But like everything else she took it in her stride, opening home and heart to welcome them.

"I worked as a midwife and a 'layer outer' — people used to come to me when they were dying or being born," she laughed, "and my husband subsidised us by doing wedding functions at the weekends — cooking and baking cakes and trifles, then we would wheel them up to the village hall in prams!"

EMIGRATED

Surrounded by her family all her life, 1963. Eight years later Peter emigrated, then Angela in 1981.

"You feel torn in two," Mum Griffiths confessed, "I wish we were all either over there or here."

Having visited Australia three times she would love to live over there permanently — but only if all her family were there too. "It was a wonderful life out there," she reminisced, "It was a beautiful country, and they really look after the elderly. — there were free cinema tickets on Wednesday mornings, with a cup of tea and cake in the interval. You could even get free hair dos as well. It was lovely."

Smiling to her self Mum Griffiths admitted to enjoying wearing shorts and ankle bracelets without attracting derogatory stares, and loving the endless rounds of outdoor barbecues. "The beaches were glorious — you looked out of place if you had any clothes on!" she laughed.

"I could be really happy out there if everyone came with me," she said. "But then everyone has to lead their own individual lives."

But wherever 'Mum Griffiths' is is certain she will continue to be living proof of the old adage 'the more you give the more you receive.'

"She is not just a mum she is a friend — everyone round her loves her, not one person has a bad word to say about her."

"My father was ambitious, but never a businessman," said Christopher explaining how his father went bankrupt after buying two cafes in Bristol but how his mum had saved the day by buying a house in her name.

Thanks to the Dursley Gazette

Before Mum died, she always said she wanted me to speak at her funeral, and often said to me 'I was the showman' and could do it. This was the hardest thing in my life to do, but I was so proud to have done it with pride and dignity, the same quality's my mother had. Everyone, my brothers, sisters and families, said how well I had talked and were so proud of me. As she was so well liked, there was hundreds at the funeral.

See my talk here.

Our Mum
Every body's Gran
95 years.
To us the best Mum in the World.
Are you ok, are you sure, she would say.
Our Mum would tell you, I'm a lucky old bird.
But all my Brothers and Sisters, twenty four grandchildren, thirty
Two great Grandchildren and one Great, Great Grandchild will tell
You we are the luckiest ones for having such a great and wonderful
Mum & Gran.
When I was a little boy growing up, I found a transparent balloon in
The fire place, now I know what it was!
It's a good job Mum & dad used them, or goodness knows how many
more brothers and sisters we would have had?
This proves that we were all planed, wanted, and loved.
We love her so much, and she loved us all.
'Butterfly in The church'
A poem our Mum liked to quote
Most of you may have heard it

'Butterfly in the Church'
Butterfly, butterfly, why come you here,
This is no bar for you go suck the honey drops sweet and clear,
Or bathe in the morning dew
This is the place to think of Heaven.
This is the place to pray.
Butterfly, butterfly,
You have no sins to be forgiven.
Butterflies fly away.
'In our Mum's own words'.
I love you all more than you'll ever know.
And I know, she knows, we love her so much too.

Born 11th April 1914, Died 4th May 2009.

There are *Angels* God puts on this Earth

Who care for us and guide us.
You can feel their love and gentleness
as they walk through life beside us.

They do great things for us every day
they whisper in our ears,
they even hold us in their hearts
when we are filled with all our fears.

They are always there to give a hug
and try to make us smile.
They treat us with respect and love,
they treat us like their child.

God blessed me with an Angel,
I'm proud to call my own.
She's been with me throughout my
life, been with me as I've grown.

She's guided me the best she can,
she's taught me like no other,
and I'm thankful I'm the lucky one
who get's to call her...

Mother

Kathleen J. Shields - May 14, 2006

Dear June and Gerald,

Moey rang me from Queensland to tell me Mrs Griffiths had died on the 4th of May, but Angela had been with her mother and all the family had time to come and say goodbye. I rang Angela in Adelaide and heard how happy she had been to spend time with her mother over the last two months and be with her when she was dying. She told me your mother had been very well cared for in the nursing home and had enjoyed being there.

The last time I saw your mother she was out staying with Sheila and celebrated her 90th birthday. I admired her courage coming half way across the world at such an age, on what is no easy trip. I will always remember her warmth and delight in all things around her, particularly people.

What a grand age and a life that spanned from the end of the Edwardian Age into the 21st century. To be born into WW1 and then live through WW11 with a husband away at sea and small children to care for, a time of great change and uncertainty. Also a world that was still filled with the horse and a few cars at the beginning of her life, but by the end, man had long landed on the moon and we now sit in our sitting rooms and look at the surface of Mars and the furthest planets without batting an eyelid. What astounding times she has lived through good and bad.

Please send my thoughts to Graham, David, Christopher and Sheila. I do not have their addresses.

June I would like to thank you for the letter you so kindly sent to me, also the note from Gerald, it was a lovely surprise. I hear from Angela you are planning to move out to Adelaide, I hope all your plans go smoothly and all the best for your new adventure/ life.

I have chosen a card that shows New Zealand's beautiful Kowhai flowers. We do not have many spectacularly coloured flowers among our native trees, but the Kowhai is one of them and it heralds the spring. Old trees can be quite large and they are covered in a mass of gold, glorious to look at. I thought your mother didn't need a sympathy card, but something that was beautiful to look at and remind one of a life that was like spring, full of hope and warmth to come. That is how I will remember Mrs Griffiths and I feel blessed to have known her.

Love

(signature)

A really nice kind letter from Jane Cook, a friend of my late brother Andrew.

It's been an emotional roller coaster these last few months, what with losing Mum as well as Angela. Angela and I hugged for our Mum, and just as Mum died Angela whispered in my ear, 'it's ok to cry'.

We talked about many things while she was over here this last time. Angela also told me what a great job Glenis and Graham had done looking after Mums needs and finances as power of attorney and executor. What with her counselling and things, she was very understanding, although she was the baby and youngest of us all. Graham, David, Christopher, Sheila, Gerald, Peter, Mary, Andrew and Angela, Angela being the youngest. She tried to help with what she could, sometimes taking charge too much.

I laid in the Hotel bed at Sydney on our way to Adelaide thinking what I could say for Angela, and just cried myself to sleep. At home Vicki rang me up crying and said 'Angela is (was) my rock what will I do now if I can't talk to her?' I know she was a rock and an inspiration to many people, especially to her Son and Daughter, Alison and Paul. When I drove her to the Airport to go home to Australia she said, 'I can't wait to get back to my babies,' meaning her Grandchildren.

She was very outspoken, especially when protecting her children, probably a little too outspoken for her own good. She would call a spade a spade and tell the truth, even of it hurt the one's she loved. But love is the main thing we as a loving family can give. Forgiveness and truth, she would come and fight in your corner. Angela was good at giving hope for someone in despair, just by being with them. It is a very great thing to have been willing to take on someone else's suffering and redeems them for us.

Mary, Andrew and Mum and Dad knew this. She was there for them, as we are here for her today.

Angela was an amazing woman. In 1991 she flew home to England from Australia and nursed my Sister Mary, who had cancer, and stayed two or three months until she died on the 11th April 1991. Years later in 2007, she went from Adelaide to Sydney in Australia to nurse my brother Andrew, who was also dying of Cancer, and stayed with him for quite a few months taking care nursing him until he died, then on the 2nd October 2007, she managed his entire funeral arrangements. She was such a strong steadfast Lady, and then when Mum had a stroke she again came straight home to see her for three months, and when our mother died before she went back to Australia, Angela spent considerable time with her, so when she went back home she was suffering from deep depression. Angela died herself a month later of a broken heart at losing Mum. If losing Mum wasn't bad enough, to lose my sister so soon after was heart breaking. My wife June and I was due to go out to Australia to activate a Visa to stay there indefinitely, and would have been living near Angela. Instead of her meeting us from the Airport, we arrived there on Monday 2nd July and went to her funeral on the Tuesday 3Rd July, she was only 57 years old and will miss her so much. She left behind a really wonderful boy friend, who she had been seeing, Carlwyn Saunders (Taff).

Rest in peace Angela, you're now with, Mary Andrew Mum and Dad, as well as young Mark.
'God Bless love you'.

This picture was taken only a months or so, before I lost them both. They will live in my heart for ever.

This is my other sister Sheila when she came home from Australia to see Mum 2009.

Dear, dear Mum on her Ninety Fifth Birthday.
In the background a picture of a young Angela.

This is a picture of Mr. David Lowe and Mum in 2009

Mr David Lowe a Radio presenter, who our mother often listen to on the Radio. She loved the sound of his voice, and I took her to Bristol B.B.C. Radio Road Show at the G1 Leisure Centre in Gloucester in England. She was so thrilled to have met him. She has rang the road show on numerous occasions and has also been on his show, where she talked to him on air. He thought the world of Mum, and used to call her Granny Griffiths.

Picture art work by Graham John Griffiths.

My memories of Mum and family, and my life, and looking back over the years.
I hope I will be able to show you all the pride and wonderful Qualities of
My Mother and Father, and those of my family.

Mum, Edith Marion Holtham.

Dad in his early twenties.

Alice Bradford Nee, Cave.

My Great, Great, Grandmother,
Mums Great Grandmother. Born Circa 1799.
Married to Cowton Bradford.
She was known as
'The Lady Cave of Bath'.

This is my Great, Great Grandfather, Cowton Bradford, and three of his brothers. As written on the back of the photo, 1st not named then Sydney and Bertrum. My Great Grandmother, and daughter of Mr Cowton Bradford, lived to the age of 99 and died in 1948, so this photo is well over two hundred years old, he is the youngest in this photograph.

Mum at 8 years old.

An Amazing picture of my Mums father, who died on the 12th April 1931. my Grandfather, Robert Fredrick Holtham.
In his Home Guard uniform, W.W.1.

This is a lovely photo of Mum aged 9 years old with her Mother Edith Minnie Holtham. It is sad as her Mother Died in 1930, just seven short years after this photo was taken, when Mum was only sixteen years old.

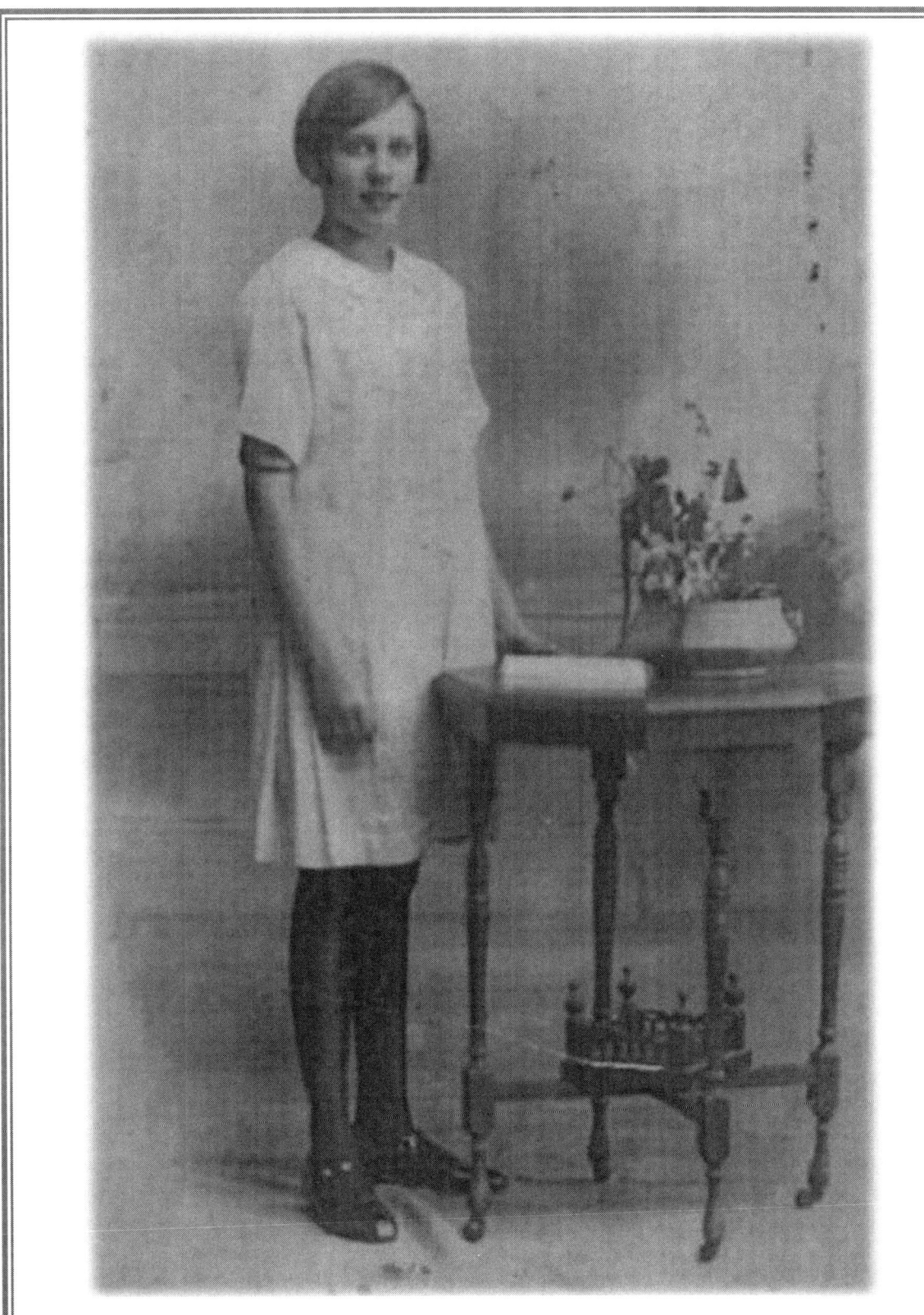

Mum at twelve years.

Mum's, Mum and Dad, Edith Minnie and Robert Fredrick Holtham.

Chapter 2

Well, where shall I start? I think it best to start by going to the very beginning, where Mum and Dad's life first began, and how my Mum met my Dad.

My Dad was born, 9th February 1911. My Mum was born 11th March 1914.

My Mother had a very privileged upbringing and attended private school and spoke the Kings English very well. The Family lived in Worle, Weston-Super-Mare. Mum being the only child of Robert Fredrick Holtham and Edith Minnie Holtham,

Mum aged 16, which was the same year she lost her Mum. Left to right: Aunty May, Mr Bruton, Mum then Aunt Violet and Cousin Joan.

Mum right aged 18 with Cousin Joan, and a Wonderful old photo of Mum with Aunty May working at the Bristol Zoo during 1933 and 1934.

Mum swimming in the sea at Weston-Super-Mare with Aunty May. Dad with his Mum & Dad at fourteen.

For a period of time Mum worked as a trainee nurse in Weston-Super-Mare General Hospital, she then moved to Brigstock Road St. Pauls to live with her Grandparents. At the age of around nineteen, Mum worked at the Bristol Zoo, where she sold trinkets and souvenirs from a kiosk, it was here working she met Dad, a Welshman.

This photo hung on the living room wall at Mum & Dads since the War years.

Mum and Dad were married in June 1934, and met at the Bristol Zoo, as they were both working there. Dad at that time was 23 years old born on the 9/2/1911 and they lived at 102 White Ladies Road Clifton Bristol.

My Grandmother Holtham, nee Bradford, Mums Mum,
She died in 1930, and looks in her forties here.

Four Brothers of my Dad, Uncle Harold, Uncle Emms, Uncle Rees, and Uncle Ernest.

With the exception of Dad and Uncle Ernest, the remainder are Pastors.

Two of Dads sisters, Aunty Alwyn, Aunty May and Mum.

Aunty May and her husband Uncle Alfred with there Grandchildren, their daughters Jean's twins, Angela & Rachel, and Jean's other daughter Elizabeth, 1966.

Granddad Thomas Bryant Griffiths front left, when Mum and Dad visited them

On their wedding day At Blackwood South Wales.

At the Back left to right: My uncle Alf, Sister Ruth, Aunty May, Cousin Jean.

My Dad, behind him is Miss Lewis, who at that time was their Servant. My Mum,

Uncle Ernie, and on the right, my Grandmother Elizabeth Emanuel Griffiths. June 5th 1934.

My Mums, Mum & Dad.   My Dads, Mum & Dad

My handsome dad, in his early Twenties.

Dad in Naval uniform, around thirty years old.

My Dad Medals.

This is the original Naval Ensign of the H.M.S. Viddet, which Dad served on during the 2nd World War.

I allowed the R.A.F. Headquarters in Quedgeley, Gloucester, Gloucestershire in England, to put it over the Bar for the Commemorative centenary celebration of the end of the 2nd World War.

H.M.S. Vidette.

Dad served in the Royal Navy, and during the War was a Petty Officer aboard HMS Bramble. The Bramble was sunk on the 31 December 1942 along with HMS Achales in the Barrent Sea's of Russia, while protecting the Russian convoys.

HMS Bramble was a Minesweeper, which was lost with all hands. Luckily, just a few days before the Bramble set sail Dad was transferred to another ship. Other ships that Dad served on were: HMS Ceto, HMS Viddett, and HMS Pintail, his first posting being HMS Ceto in August 1941, and spent only a short period on that Ship. He was transferred to the small HMS Bramble, protecting the Russian convoys, from the Bramble he was transferred to HMS Viddett.

My Brother David Griffiths has written a book about the memories of the loved ones that died when the Bramble went down, which is dedicated to their memory. The book is called, 'Passages from The Past'. For more information on this book, go to: or if you are reading this on your computer click here.

www.hms-bramble-crew.talktalk.net/

The H.M.S Bramble.

In the War's of the World , whether it be on land sea or air, there were so many lives lost, they do say in the name of freedom. I do agree with that, but most of the tragedies and loss of life in conflicts throughout the world, are all to do with money, greed and power of governments and religions. They are the heads of power in governments and the religious inquisitions that have destroyed the lives of people throughout centuries. But, without the bravery of the fighting men, which incidentally are the real men that are fighting for their country and freedom, which includes my father and many like him fighting for the security of their loved ones, these are the real hero's. Although I went into the forces myself, I never ever went through the terrible hardships these young men had gone through.

The admiration and respect for these men should never go unrecognised and even a thought for the men of the enemy that also fought bravely, they were only doing the best for their country and what they thought was right.

In the cold Antarctic waters, there were many battles between ships, some are well known as is the bravery of the men and of the many thousands that lost their lives from the terrible threat of death lurking U-boats. As I have just written about my Dad and the ships he has sailed on during the Antarctic Wars, this is why I wanted to put these feelings down. The battle where the Bismark sunk HMS Hood before being sunk itself by Swordfish from the famous British Carrier HMS Ark Royal.

P.O. Morgan Griffiths had served on HMS Bramble for some time, but was transferred to another ship, HMS Viddett. Shortly after this event, HMS Bramble set sail on its ill fated trip to the Barrens Seas of the Russian waters and whilst escorting Convoy JW518 was damaged by the German Battleship Hipper, then later sunk with the loss of all hands by the German Destroyer Eckholdt. That day, the 31st December 1942, a total of 8 Officers and 113 ratings went down with their ship, Dad could so well have been one of them!

My brother David felt so passionate about the stories our Dad had told him, especially at how he had lost all his mate's during the sinking of the HMS Bramble. Since the death of our Father, David has had a project of compiling stories from the relatives of those that died on the Bramble, who had kindly sent him stories of the ship and their loved one's that never came back. He had a huge response, and as a result was able to bring out a book of stories from all the relatives of the crew that died, which is a great tribute to both him, and them.

Morgan, Dad in the front with some of his shipmates on the H.M.S Bramble.

H.M.S Bramble.

H.M.S Ark Royal.

Going forward in time to the 7th April 2010, which was the day I received a visitor, a Mr. Erick white and wife Jenny to my home. I had previously met them a few days earlier whilst visiting the Seymore cafe in Gloucester, and felt a need to add his story to this part of my book.

I had invited Erick and Jenny to my home, and during the conversation he informed me of his father, Idris Rubin White, who during the Second World War had served with the Fleet Air Arm, aboard H.M.S Ark Royal and H.M.S Hood.

As the conversation was about the Ark Royal, I thought it would be interesting to put these Photo's in this story, as they are not only interesting, they are photos his father had actually taken himself. One of these photo's show H.M.S Ark Royal in a dry dock in Japan, where the ship was actually held up by bamboo canes. Thousands of tonnes just held up by bamboo!

There is also a beautiful shot of the ship at sea, plus one of the H.M.S Hood. Although my Dad had nothing to do with the Ark Royal, or the Hood, I found it so interesting to have had the privilege of talking to Mr. White, and decided to include these two photographs for other people to see.

This is of course a famous ship, and we need to remind the world of the courage and great Battles and Honours of this and other ships, plus the brave men aboard that had given their lives, and should not forget their bravery and contribution to the War effort. The memory of these men must live on, especially at Remembrance Days, so the next generations will not forget they gave their live, so we could be free, from dictatorship and persecution of foreign lands.

H.M.S Hood.

H.M.S Ark Royal in dry-docks in Japan.

Note: All the Bamboo canes holding the ship up.

This is why I wanted to put his story in my book.
Top of the picture is Mr. Idris Rubin White, waving.

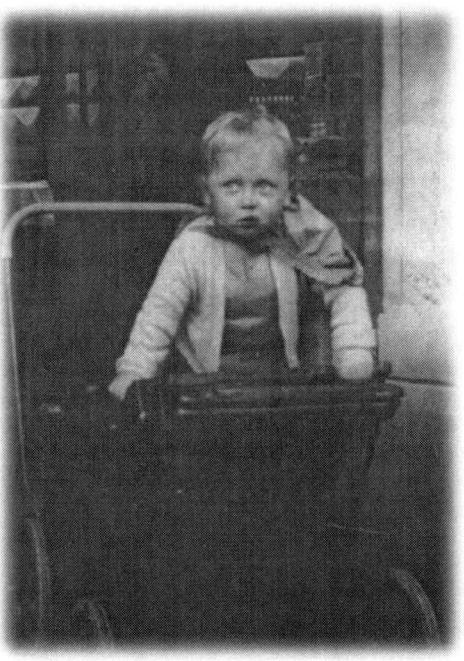

This is Graham, my eldest brother in both photo's about eight months old.

At the outbreak of War in 1939 Mum had four children, Graham, David, Christopher and Sheila. As the war progressed, so the family grew, and by the end of the war they had two more, Gerald, that's me, and Peter.

I was the fifth child and one of nine children to Edith Marion & Morgan Griffiths, these were: Graham, David, Christopher, Sheila ,Gerald, (that's me) Peter, Mary, Andrew and Angela. (Ha-ha so I must have been the fifth twinkle in my Dad's eye). There were, six boys and three girls.

Left to right: Graham, Christopher, David and Sister Sheila.

Mum gave birth to me on the living room floor, they built them tough in those days, and she was such a great lady, she was loved and like by everyone that knew her. As I said she was tough, and throughout the years, brought up nine children, of which we all turned out for the good. By the time I had gone to school Mum had three more children, Mary, Andrew and Angela. Three month before I was born, in August 1941, Dad left to go aboard H.M.S Ceto, Mum was all alone.

I was born 10th November 1941 in Bristol, Number 9 Sunnydene Road, on the Sutton Estate in Brislington in Bristol. Six of us were born during the War years, and a couple of years before my brother Peter was born, when I would have only been around four or five months old, our house received a direct hit from a German Luftwaffe Bomb, on the 26th April 1942.

The Bomb went straight through the middle of the roof, destroying our home and next door. At the sound of Sirens, Mum always got us out of bed and into the Air Raid Shelter. Some people became complacent and did not bother, lucky for us Mum was not one of those, the Air Raid Shelter was in our garden, just a few yards from the house. Mum and I, plus my three brothers and sister, had to be virtually dug out.
I was in a carry-cot and covered in soot, they thought I was dead. But we were so lucky to be alive. We lost everything and during that time Dad was away at sea.
As Mum was by herself at the time of the bombing, Dad was allowed home on Compassionate leave.

Dad on his first leave after I was born. Mum Dad, myself & my sister Sheila. 1942.

When the family home was bombed, we were dug out of the shelter and taken to Gloucestershire. Here we were put in a place for homeless families, and recovered in tents on the Badminton Estate, called The Queen Mary Home at Hinnegar Camp. As I was so young, I have no memory of this yet I do have a vague memory of Mum holding me up to the upper floor window in Sunnydean showing me the Barrage Balloons over the Docks, which would help keep the bombers away. This was after the house was rebuild and we went home,

As I had said, I was about four to five months old, and while we were there Queen Mary visited the Camp. She had seen me being held by my Mum and asked to hold me. She said I had a wobbly head, probably became she was not holding me properly. She returned on another visit and asked to see the baby with the wobbly head, and everyone began running around trying to find Mum to bring me to the Queen.

That was my first encounter with Royalty, it would not be the last!

The Queen Mary at Hinnagar Camp for homeless families, I am in Mums arms, top left.

The Queen Mary was born on 26th May 1867 and died peacefully after illness on the 24th March 1953. She was laid to rest at Windsor, and buried alongside her husband H.R.H King George V, in St George's Chapel Windsor. She lived at The Gloucestershire Estate of Badminton. She was a steadfast lady, with a strong sense of duty through both World Wars. She was enduring and affectionate with every one she met.

Chapter 3.

From the home for homeless families we were re - housed in Bloomfield Road Bristol. The family returned to No 9 Sunnydene after it was completely rebuilt, and later joined by Dad, back from the war, and not in the best of health.
This is Mum and Dad after the War, starting from the top down: Graham, David, Christopher, Sheila then me and Peter. In front of the Air-raid Shelter that saved our Lives. I am in the Front Left.

The Hinnegar Camp on the Badminton Estate near Chipping Sodbury.

These two photos were taken when we lived at Sunnydean Road. Brislington on the Sutton Estate and Angela was the last to be born there at Brislington.

This is Angela sitting on the step outside No 9, and one of her taken at a studio in Bristol. Not long after we moved to the Cafe in the centre of Bristol.

I can remember when we were moving to the Cafe. Christopher, Peter and myself went by bus and we had all these clothes on instead of carrying them, we also had other clothes with us packed in suitcases. We were sitting on the Bus sweating like anything as it was summer and had some weird looks from the passengers and the Bus Conductor. The Bus Stop was at the top of our road on the Wick Road, and was about twenty to forty-fifty minute drive into town, then a little walk to the Cafe.

Sunnydean Road as it is today in 2010, and the new sign in the photo on the wall, they have spelt wrong! I do know this for a fact, that is why someone pencilled in an 'N'. All the houses have been rebuilt fairly recently. To think that when our house was rebuilt, we were the first people on the Sutton Estate to have an inside bathroom and toilet, lots of people came to have a look around.

Before the bombing, Mum used to boil the water in the copper wash tub and bath us standing up in that. None of the houses had bathrooms, instead they had to boil the water on a gas stove and use a tin bath in the living room, then put it outside in the shed when finished. All rooms had open fireplaces and it used to get really cold in the winter, as in those days, there was no such thing as central heating. So you can imagine how hard it was for Mum when she gave birth to me all alone by the fire on the living room floor on a cold November day.

This 1930's baby in a miniature version of the family tin bath, an adult's bath would be the same shape but much longer. The bath was called a Zinc Bath and was made of galvanised iron. Once the bath was filled, we all had to take a bath one after the other to save on the water. This was because of having no facilities of fresh hot water every time for each person, you can imagine the later privilege of being able to have an actual bathroom with running hot water.

The End of the War celebration street party.
David standing next to Graham, Christopher, Gerald & Peter on the Table in the foreground.
Sheila next to David Wright on the table behind in the middle centre.

The Infants & Junior School I attended at the top of Bloomfield road.

This is the gate at Bloomfield Road Infants School, the Gate I trapped my finger in.

'I do believe these are now listed buildings'.

When I was around five or six, I managed to trap my finger in these gates, which can be seen in this photo, and almost cut the top of my finger off, there was blood everywhere! what happened, was some of the other children were holding the gate shut, so I could not get in, I managed to get it opened some way, then they pulled it back slamming it shut and trapping my finger. I was taken to hospital where I was treated, and still bare the scar to this day.

We used to go to Sunday School when we live in Sunnydean, and across the road from that was an ice-cream parlour. Mum would give us some small change for the collection at the bible class, but us children used to go over the ice-cream parlour and buy ice-cream instead. One day, Mr. Tarr, the owner, who knew mum, gave me a big tub of ice-cream to give mum. He knew we were a large family, and his fridges had broken down, he did not want to waste any of it. On the way home I ate half of it, that day I was so ill, and sick. I think God was punishing me for spending our collection money on ice-cream. The Ice-cream parlour is still there to this very day.

This is the Ice-Cream Parlour.   The old Langton Court Pub is still there to this day.

This Bridge down by the Feader Canal is still there and we as children used to climb right up over the parapit you see in these pictures, children as they say have no fear. Mum would of had a fit if she knew what we got up to.

Langton Court Railway Bridge, next to my school. We used to play on this as well, which doesn't bear thinking about! We had to amuse ourselves somehow, and when we were small there was no Television or computures in our day. I can remember running home from School, just to listen to special agent 'Dick Barton' and 'Journey's into space' on the radio.

When we, that is my Brother Peter and I went to junior school, we used to go sledging in the Summer on the grassy bank of a large hayfield, and remember sledging one weekend at a place we called the Hayfields. We use to make a sledge and candle-wax the runners, which made it go really fast as the grass became very shinny and slippery. We had great fun there, Mother would pack us some lunch and we would stay there all day long, but she also warned us to be back before the street lights came on.

Anyway, on to my story. While we were playing a boy stopped by, who seemed to be looking for trouble. I don't now remember what it was all about, but think it was because he was firing a pellet gun at us. Anyway, this boy then picked a fight with Peter and came off worst. Although others wanted to get involved it was a stand up fight between the two of them and somehow I managed to keep the fight between Peter and this boy.

Although we were not looking for trouble, it was the other boy that started the fight and this incident happen outside of school hours. However, the following day saw the boy's parents turn up at the school and demanded Peter was punished. We did quite rightly state the boy had started the trouble, but the Headmistress still caned Peter in front of the entire school during assembly while the boys parent looked on, and our parents were not consulted at all.

When Mum found out she was furious! My sister Sheila, who had recently left school, told her she would go up there and give the Headmistress a piece of her mind, as this incident should have been dealt with by the parents and certainly not have involved the school as the event happened outside the school working hours.

We used to go down the Hayfields, where a bridge crossed the stream at the bottom and go fishing for Tiddlers, Sticklebacks and which we called Redbreasts (which is Redthroats. Did you know Redthroats are adult male Sticklebacks? and after they mate they die!) as well as tadpoles ECT. The photo of Peter shows him at around four years old and much younger than when the above incident occurred.

When I went to the Wick Road Secondary Modern School, all in Brislington, as Dad was a chef, and after a period of working at Mardens, Dad had received his severance pay, and with this, we moved in 1953 to the centre of Bristol, where are parents opened a restaurant in Dyton Street. We ended up having two cafes' there. Mum and Dad and all the family worked long hours to make the business's work but sadly, due to the Bristol Council wanting to rebuild and redirect the road, plus adding yellow lines, the restaurant was bought on a Compulsory Purchasing Order and their business's came to an end.

When we moved to the Restaurant, I then went to School up on Kings Down Parade, and stayed at the same School until I left for work aged fifteen.

We then moved to Number One Southernhay Road Clifton. This house was high up on a bank overlooking the Docks where the S.S. Great Britain now stands. I had two Jobs, the first working for a builder, the second working for the Bristol Corporation as a Plumbers Mate, and with a Stonemason.

No 1 Southernhay Road.   No 74 Sandy Park Road.

This is the Bristol Docks as it was then, where the S.S. Great Britain now stands. When we lived at Southernhay Road our house was just in through the gap that you see at the top of the picture, which overlooks the dock. We were not there for very long and from Clifton, Mum and Dad moved back to Brislington, to No 74 Sandy Park Road, and is where we lived when I enlisted for the forces, (as you will learn later).

Many of my teenage years were spent there and I used to love going Dancing. There was a big dancehall up on the Downs near Clifton called the Glen Ballrooms. I used to love Jiving and Rock-&-Roll, and would go most Friday nights. Here I met a girl named Susan Taylor, and went out with her for a year or so. As a teenager I thought I was in love, but she led me a merry dance, and in general messed me around two-timing me and was always getting me into fights because of her, and to cut a long story short, decided to end the relationship. There is another story concerning this/here later in the book.

Left to right: Peter and Mum, Andrew, Gerald at Sandy Park Road. I was about sixteen or seventeen.

Gerald at nineteen. People use to say I looked like James Dean.

Little story about Lady Smyth

and my Mum, Edith Marion Griffiths Nee, Holtham.

At the Ashton Court Estate in Long Ashton.

When my Mum was about six years old and up to about eighteen, she told me she was a regular visitor to, The Lady Smyth's Estate in Long Ashton Court. My Mum used to go from Weston-Super-Mare to Lady Smyth's Estate by horse drawn carriage as her parents, Robert Fredrick Holtham, and Edith Minnie Holtham, were very close friends of Lady Smyth, and on several occasions The Late King George V was there. Mum told us she often sat on his knee on numerous occasions during the festivities.

I have since learned from being in the Grenadier Guards, that Mum would have been classed as a Debutant, within the upper-class, you could say that both her, as well as her parents were socialist's. Mum had a privileged upbringing, and in today's society would be classed as jetsetter's, or the jet set. I do believe this is more than likely where she met and began walking out with a Major Germaine, then serving with the Coldstream Guards. Mum told me this and the story goes that while he was serving abroad in India, she then met Dad and started going out with him. While he was away Major Germaine had asked mum to look after his Red Coldstream Guards Ceremonial Tunic. However, one day, whilst Mum was entertaining Dad in the Parlour, her mother entered the room, and whispered to her that the Major was at the door. Without dad knowing, she took his Tunic to him and finished with him that night, eventually marrying my Dad in June of 1934.

The beautiful gracious home of lady Smyth, Ashton Court Estate was an easily accessible historic estate only two miles from the Bristol City Centre, and has magnificent old oak trees and has had deer grazing in the grounds of the estate for over six hundred years.

However in 1939 it was requisition by the War Office, and was used as a Transit Camp and R.A.F H.Q. It was also an American Command H.Q. Lady Smyth died in 1946, and with the house already in disrepair it then laid empty for a further 13 years. Over the years, dry rot, damp and vandalism had played their part of its dilapidation. It was then in 1959 that the Bristol City Council purchased the house from Greville Cavendish.

This is where I came in! It's quite ironic, because after hearing Mum's stories of Lady Smyth, I was working for the City Council at the Bristol Corporation in Meadow Street. At the time I was working with a Stonemason named Mr. O'Connell, who had been instructed to remove a window from the Lady Smyth's Estate before it got damaged by vandals. This was a beautiful window depicting the crucifixion of Christ on a Cross, with Mary and the disciple's underneath, kneeling in prayer.

This is a picture of the top centre window where we removed the glass panels as it is today, but I seem to remember it being much larger, this wall seem's to have been rebuilt. The other picture is the beautiful carved stairway leading to the floor where the window was.

The Coat of Arms of the Smyth family who owned Ashton Court from 1545 to 1959.
The motto translated: 'He who Rules by the sword, shall be slain by the sword'.

This picture allows you to see how Grandeur everything was and how it would have looked in its day.

Now it has all been renovated, you can see the beautiful woodwork of its carvings.

To enable us to remove the window in one piece, we had scaffolding erected on the outside, and also had to work on the inside, and believed the window was to be taken to the Bristol Museum. There were also one or two other windows that had to be removed, but if memory serves me right, these were not as large. This work took almost two weeks, and during my lunch break I often went off to exploring around the old empty house.

I can remember the Winter Garden that had become all dilapidated with its entire glass roof smashed, and the beautiful terra cotta tiles ripped up from the floor. Some of the rooms were huge with big fireplaces, and on the top of these was the family crest. I remember finding a small door in one of the big ballrooms, which could not have been any more than a few feet off the floor. It was locked, and in some of my lunch breaks, would try and unlock it with a piece of wire. After several attempts over the next few days, I managed to open this door and found a spiral staircase leading up towards the roof. I then found another locked door, which I also managed to open.

Inside I found a photographic dark room, with lots of cameras and photographic equipment on the floor. On the table near the window were a few hundred photographic glass plates, and on these was able to recognise King George V with a lady, which I assumed was Lady Smyth. These plates appeared to be rather personal, and on my return informed Mr. O'Connell, who also came to view them, then went off and rang the office. Within the hour the C.I.D. arrived with several Tea Chest's, which they placed the items in and took them away. Looking back: If only I had taken one, I would now be very wealthy.

That was the last we heard about this incident.

'The Lady Smyth's Estate, Ashton Court Mansion'. Now called: 'Ashton Court Estate'.

My wife June and I, had recently returned from obtaining photographs and researching items at The Lady Smyth's Ashton Court on 16 April 2010. On the way there, I called at one of the childhood places where I used to play, this was a place called Abbots Leigh.

This is along the road after you pass Lady Smyth's on the Clevedon Road after going over the Clifton Suspension Bridge. From Ashton Court, you travel along this road towards Abbots Leigh, here you turn left into Manor Road. Keep on this road until you see a sign for the pool, then turn right onto the off road track. Here everything is signed, including the Car Park. As well as being a place of much history, it is also a place of much beauty, here we used to swim and play in the pool.

As rumour would have it, it is supposed to be haunted by a Monk that was said to be murdered by a fellow monk, who drowned him in the pool, or should I say this was the tale we heard from those living in and around Abbots Leigh. But I wonder if any of that was actually true?

We used to go there all the year round, especially during the different seasons, and would often go camping in the autumn and collect sweet Chestnuts and Conkers. There were also hoards of beautiful flowers to brighten the day from Rhododendron's, and Bluebells (*Hiyacinthoides non-scripta*) during April to early June. From May to July there are beautiful Flags Iris's (*Iris Pseudacorus*), with their sword like leaves which formed large clumps beside the water's edge.

Sometimes the water would be covered with Water-lily *(Nughar luea)* and these would bloom and appear from June to August. These had massive underground stems, which would anchor themselves to the bottom of the pool, while their leaves and flowers would grow up through the water and float to the surface. This pool was teeming with life. Dragonfly's Southern Hawker (*Aeshna cyanea*) and would fly from late October, Pheasants, King Fisher's, as well as a multitude of other birds and wildlife would also come there to drink.

We would often swing from a rope over the pool, sometimes quite high, or run down through the woods and dive off a convenient cave, diving clear of the ground then entering the pool.

While I was there on this recent visit, I wondered how on earth we ever managed to do that. I will never know, the cave seemed so far from the pool, and to dive over that amount of ground, seemed almost impossible. But looking back, it appears children have no fear. 'See cave and pool in the photo', you'll see what I mean.

This pool cave was originally built as a Boathouse. Just look at the distance the cave is from the pool! It doesn't bear thinking about. I can only assume the cave entrance has moved, because of dilapidation, or they may have rebuilt the bank since I was a Child.

Abbots Pool a brief history. As from the Middle Ages, these pools were used by the Monks from St Augustine's Abbey in Bristol to provide fresh fish, Tench (*Tinca-tinca*) when they were staying at a rest-house, while the tracks that run through the woodlands are thought to date back to the Roman era.

In the 1920's, the woodlands and pools were in the possession of Walter Melvelle Wills who had the area enhanced by a well known landscaping company named James Pulham & Son's. There was also a dam, cascade and cave.

The Pulham-mix. This is an artificial material made from a mixture of concrete and local stone, and was used in the gardens at Buckingham Palace as well as other stately homes. Most likely some of the stonework was used on the Lady Smyth's estate. The recent restoration work has been funded by the Heritage Lottery Fund, and now belongs to the North Somerset Council.

The Clifton Suspension Bridge, Bristol.

My wife June and I had recently returned from a trip today to the Clifton Suspension Bridge. We had gone there to take some photographs of the Bridge; this is to allow you to understand more clearly the event that happened when I was a young man of sixteen.

An Aeroplane flying under the Clifton Suspension Bridge.

The plane flew from right to left under the bridge in this picture.

On or around 1957, I can remember playing with my brother Peter along the Port Way under the Clifton Suspension Bridge. On the far side of the Avon Gorge is Leigh Woods alongside the railway tracks, and here we used to play, as well as walking all along the Port Way. On this particular day, as we made our way along this track, we were surprised to see a low flying airplane coming towards us from the Ashton side of the bridge, and watched as it did just that. We could not believe it! It was going to fly under the bridge! when it came out the other side it then flipped upside down and came around again. We later found out the manoeuvre was a Victory Roll. After that, the plane started to go out of sight and around the curve of the gorge where it briefly reappeared before crashing into the side of the gorge.

Having seen this, we started to run along the towpath to where it now lay. There was debris everywhere, and by the time we got there the Fire Brigade turned up and told us to move back. I have since been able to go on the internet, and find details of the person involved in this incident. Apparently, the Officer who had flown the plane was Pilot Flying Officer John Greenwood Crossley aged only 27 years old, and was based at Filton and was flying a De Havilland Vampire Jet. When he flew under the bridge and performed his slow roll, he then entered clouds, where we lost sight of him for a moment and would assume that was when everything went wrong for him. He then remerged inverted and rolled, turning towards Leigh Woods he rapidly lost even more height, and struck the side of the gorge.

The exact date was 3rd of February 1957. It is said this was most likely an act of suicide as his speed was far too high at 450 miles an hour and would (should?) have been nearer 250 knots.

The De Havilland Vampire jet.

The View of the bridge.

This picture is where the plane started its approach to the bridge.

This memory will stay with me forever. When we first saw him crash there was a loud bang and large puffs of smoke, we could see the smoke as we ran to where it happened, which was a good way from the Bridge from where we were at the time it went under, and by the time we reached the crash site, it was only a short time when the fire Brigade arrived.

The view from the Bridge showing the direction the plane came from.

In the photo above, if my memories are correct, the plane crashed just past out of sight on the left bank, where the last bend jut's out.

His was the last flight by anyone passing under the bridge.

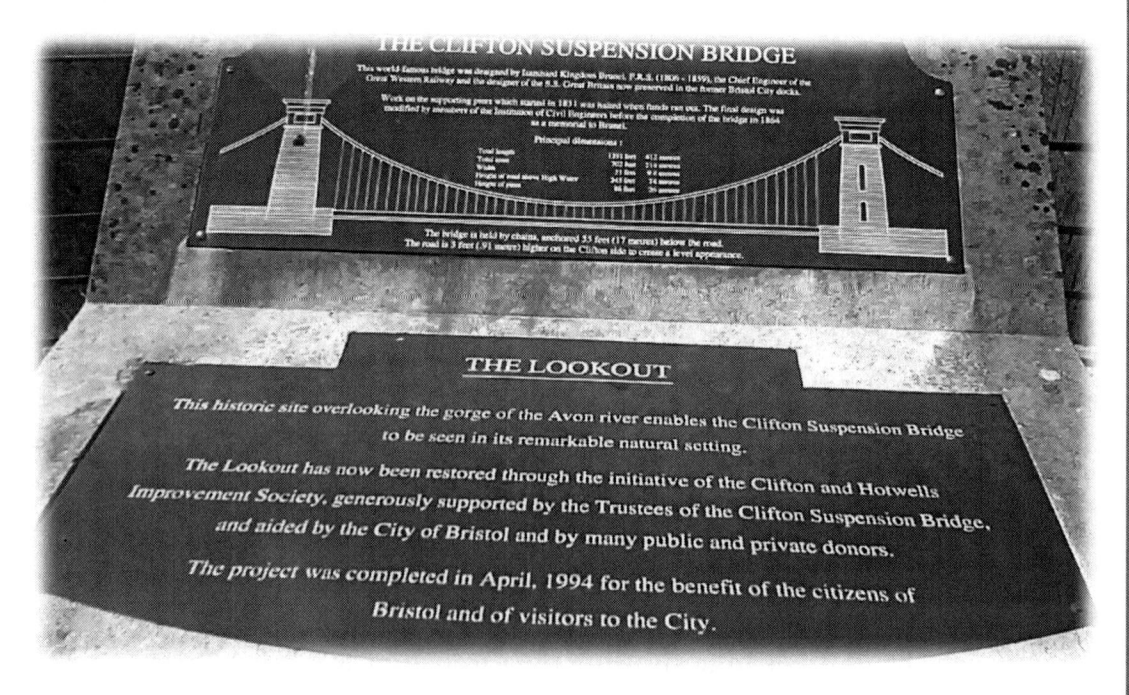

This is a stone notice near the Bridge.

The road named Port Way was opened in 1931. At that time it was said to be the most expensive road per mile and travels the entire length of the gorge. On the Leigh Woods side of the river, the old Bristol to Portishead Railway once ran, and traces of this can still be seen to the present day, even though it was closed in the 1960's. For those passing along this old line there were, and still are, several old tunnels which the Train's from a bygone age once passed through. The trees from Leigh Woods sit happily above and small underpasses below the railway, which were once entrances to the Leigh Woods, and places of my childhood memories.

Going under these Railway lines into the Leigh Woods, there were recesses in the cliff face resembling small quarries, where Tramps and homeless people had once built little camps of sheds and shelters and on many occasions, although they were living very rough, both my Brother and I would call and share a cup of tea with them,. I recall a couple, but not their names, that once lived there, who invited us into their small cosy shack, complete with a nice warming fire, and enjoyed their hospitality.

During the Spring, we often went along there picking flowers to take home to our Mum. There was a great variety and often picked Bluebells along with all manner of other flowers. By going on the internet, during my research, I've since learned many of these flowers are of rare species that are only native to the gorge and nowhere else in the world. There is the Flower of Bristol which is named the, (*Lychnis Chalcedonica,*) the Bristol Onion and the White-Beam which can grow up to thirty feet tall, as well as a plant named the Squill.

The Bristol Onion plant.   **The Squill plant from the Gorge.**

This picture was taken from a viewing esplanade on the Downs. In the photo you can see the Suspension Bridge in the distance, and on the right edge of the river you can just see the towpath amongst the trees, where the airplane crashed. Up until the 16th April 2010, I did not visualise how big the Downs were, and of course when you are young and look back in later years, it is hard to remember all the little things you have done in your life. As I explored, it really was déjà-vu, I really thought I had done all this before 'weird', but it was great fun and brought back many happy memories, it even brought back memories of when Dad worked at the Bristol Zoo, which is on the side of the Downs.

Bristol Zoo was only a stone's throw from the esplanade where I took the photo of the Clifton Suspension Bridge, and if you travel a mile along this road, you will arrive opposite the main entrance to the Zoo, and on this same day, we called there and took this picture.

The main entrance to the Bristol Zoo.

This is the side entrance, where we used to enter the Zoo.

The kitchens are to the left of the window. Mum often took us to the Zoo to see Dad when he was working and used the side entrance to the rear of the kitchens where he worked, so used to get in for free.

While our parents were together, us children used to run off collecting discarded lemonade bottles from the ground and litter bins, then return them to the Zoo Shop to receive the deposit on them. In those days I believe it was two or three old pennies for each of them. As there were twelve Pennies to the Shilling, and twenty Shillings to the Pound, this we found most profitable, and by the end of the day we would often go home with six or seven Shillings between us which in those days was a handsome sum of money, especially as the average weekly pay for adults was only around six or seven Pounds.

This is Mum on the Downs at Clifton. Left to right: Christopher, Mary, Mum, Andrew, and Sheila, and Mum was probably on her way to the Zoo to see Dad.

Not long after, while I was working for the Bristol Corporation and living at 74 Sandy Park Road, I went into the Armed Forces, more of that later. Mum and Dad then moved to Slimbridge Church in Slimbridge.

This picture was taken outside Slimbridge Church House. Mum and Dad, my Brother Graham's oldest two children, Shaun and Mark, plus our two dogs, Kim and Suzy.

Dearest Dad and Angela, at the Church house, Slimbridge.

Our son Graham sitting on the grass, Angela, standing, then Sarah, Mary's daughter, Paul sitting on Granny Griffiths's lap, then Alison. Paul & Alison being Angela's son & daughter. Second picture: Graham with Angela and her children Alison & Paul.

Mum was the Verger in Slimbridge Church House. She used to look after the Village Hall, which was attached to our house. The next move was to the canal, still in Slimbridge, where Dad worked as a Bridgeman, on British Waterways. Mum loved having us there so much. It was here the family had so many happy times together, we would all gather there as a family by the bank.

Mum reading a story to Graham & Sarah.   In this picture, standing Kevyn and Alison, sitting, Marie, Paul, and Jonny. Kevin, Marie and Jonny being Christopher's three children.

David & June at the rear, then Janet, Mum, Debby, and Gerald with his dog Mandy. This picture Sarah & Vicki.

When Mum lived here she worked down the road at the Slimbridge Wildfowl Trust. She met Sir Peter and Lady Scot on several occasions. She also met the Duke of Edinburgh, and the Queen has visited on numerous occasions, plus Mum has actually met Prince Charles whilst there, and sat talking to him while he had his lunch. Dad loved this job, and was so happy there. Being a chef he would help out at the pub just across the road. This pub was called the Tudor Arms, highly recommended for great food.

This is my dad opening the Patch Bridge, at Slimbridge.

Later in my book you will find I also became a Bridgeman on Waterways.

Mark and Debbie. Graham's two children, on the canal bank at Slimbridge. Mum and Dad's house is in background. When Mum and Dad lived there, I used to come home on leave from the army, and hitch-hiked home in my uniform, which would be unheard of today for security reasons, and most soldiers would now have a car anyway. I am just about to get to that part about the Army.

Dad with Mark, Shaun and Debbie, by the Slimbridge Bridge.

Mark and Graham with two German friends on our Boat.

This is Dad, and you would not believe it, he actually cut this car up with a hacksaw blade, for Peter, because he could not take it down to the scrap yard, he cut it up and put it in the dustbin every week until it had gone. This was no small car, it was a large American, Ford Fairlane.

Dad loved a drink, but not to excess and loved to socialise. As you can see he loved to throw a dart. Mum & Dads next move was to Arlington, near Frampton on Severn in the Lodge House doing domestic chores for Lady Dent. Mum loved it but Dad didn't due to the three mile walk to get a Pint at the pub.

During this time, when Mum was working at Lady Dents and was waiting on her guest's, she learnt that the guest's names were Coronel and Lady Gray 'cheap, which was the mother and father of my Platoon Commander when I served with the Grenadier Guards. You will learn more about this a little further on in the book. They then moved to Dursley, No 1 Tyndale Road Woodfields. This is where my parents lived, when we lost our Dad.

My Dear dad died on the 24th October 1978. He had a pacemaker for a few years, and died of a heart attack, which was quick. We miss him very much and Mum never ever wanted anybody else. Mum stayed at Woodfields until 2007 then she went to the retirement home at the Old Vicarage at Frampton on Severn. This is the home where we lost Mum 4th May 2009.

Mum, 11th March 1914 ------- 4th May 2009.   Dad, 9 February 1911 ---24th October 1978.

This is a wonderful picture of Graham left & Glenis at their wedding and Brother David.

Still at Slimbridge. left to right are: Peter, Mum, Dad, Uncle Ernie, his wife Dorothy.

To the rear: Janet and David and two of their girls to the front, Annette, and Julie.

Our wonderful Mum and Dad.

Chapter (4)
Gerald Griffiths
When he Served In
The Grenadier Guards

THE RECORD OF MILITARY SERVICE

OF GERALD GLYN GRIFFITHS

WHO SERVED WITH THE

THE GRENADIER GUARDS

FROM 1ST AUGUST 1961

UNTIL 31ST JULY 1970

DISCHARGED 31ST JULY 1973

SERVICE NUMBER 23862933

RANK LANCE/CORPORAL

FOR CROWN AND COUNTRY

Gerald Griffiths's medals

Gerald in Beret with cap badge, a Grenadier Grenade thrown Proper.

Going back to when we lived at Sandypark Road Brislington in 1961 and before moving to Slimbridge, I made the biggest decision of my life, and that decision was to join the Army!

I chose a very tough regiment, my life changed so dramatically and I became a man. My parents were so proud of me, especially when I first came home dressed in my uniform.

I did learn later that Mum went out with a Guards Officer from the Coldstream Guards, before she met my Dad, which I already explained.

I had enlisted into The Grenadier Guards. This is great, because the Grenadier's are the most senior regiment in the British army, and being bayous and all?

From the actual day of walking into the Recruiting Office, I had a medical and received my Travel Warrant to get me to the Guards Depot in the space of only three days! 'Well,' I thought,' that's it!'

But when I finally arrived on the Friday afternoon, they said they had no idea why we'd been sent, as the Camp was going on two weeks block, leave. I was gutted! They then sent us all back home, that is all the new recruits that had arrived that weekend. We also had an added bonus of receiving two weeks pay and another Travel Warrant, and all this before I'd done anything remotely military.

Sheila, Gerald's sister at 22 years old, and Gerald at 20 years old at Sandy Park just before he went into the Grenadier Guards. Both these photos were taken same time and place.

Home on my first leave from the Guards Depot after being in only two days.

Mum & myself with my Dog 'Kim' **1961**.

When I arrived back home, Mum and Dad didn't believe me. My oldest brother, who had been in the army thought I had gone A.W.O.L. (Absent Without Leave). But managed to convince them my story was true. Incidentally, three of my older brother served their National Service; I had missed this by two years, but decided to enlist anyway. When I first enlisted it was for six years, but later in my career, because the money was better, I added a further three years and made it a total of nine years.

This seemed the longest two weeks of my life, just killing time and waiting to go back. When I eventually returned to the Guards Depot, training started almost immediately. Much of this training was spent pounding around the barrack square, marching at a great rate of knots!

To give you an idea of how fast we had to march, if we were marching to music it would be as fast as the old Rock-&-Roll rhythm of, One Two Three O'clock, four O'clock Rock, around 140 paces a minute, or faster. As well as rifle drill, we also went to the gym at least twice a day, plus much running through the woods and firing our rifle's on one of the many ranges.

A few weeks into our training we all were on the bayonet assault course, which consisted of a rather large sand hill. We had to run up to the top, then on through the woods to the start where the assault course had numerous nets and obstacles to navigate. Some were nets and planks to run across, nets to crawl under and climb, and nets to swing from one plank to another, this over water. Some of these were high in the trees, and to balance as you passed over these obstacles proved rather difficult.

On completing the Assault Course we came out of the woods and ran back to the start, which proved rather difficult as the track running alongside the range consisted of loose sand and was difficult to run on.
When we got to this sandy part we thought no one would be there to see us. But, the Trained Soldiers would be waiting and kept us moving. Then it was back to the sand hill at the start and do it all over again. This we would do around nine or ten times in one session.

When I returned to the barrack room after being dismissed I went to the toilet, locked myself in one of the cubicles, and burst into tears. This was mostly from fatigue and utter exhaustion. But, while I was there, I heard someone sobbing in the next cubical and silently stood on the seat and slowly looked over the dividing wall. Here I saw another young Guardsman in much the same state as myself!
Quickly drying my eyes, I silently left the toilets and made my way back to the barrack room. The person I'd seen considered himself something of a tough guy, an ex Merchant Navy person covered in tattoo's.
After that, I vowed never to feel like that again, and was a turning point as it toughened me up.
When he returned I remarked, 'the assault course was great fun, wasn't it?' and never let on I'd seen or heard him crying.

This is the sand hill we had to run up. We used to do this about ten times, then along the top, down through the woods, over the obstacles, return alongside the ranges and back again up the hill.

The Grenadier Guard's Depot Pirbright. L/Cpl Wright's Squad, 1961.

Rear Rank; Gdsm. A. Bosson. G. Griffiths. J. Harrison. M. Peacey. M.Bullion. A. Ince. G. Oldfield. G. Lloyd

Centre Rank; Gdsm. C. Beck. R.Dobson. J. Masterman. K. Phillips. R. Choules. K. King. R. Knight R. Bond. A. Craven.

Front Rank; Gdsm. K. Tatton. L/Sgt. K. Fielding. (Gym training Instructor)C.S.M. Brackenbridge. Maj. P.J.C. Ratcliffe. (Coy Commander) L/Cpl. R. Wright. (Sqd Instructor) Lf. R.G. Proes. Sgt. C. Lovell. (Subt Sgt) T/Sdr. G. Lock. (Sqd Instructor)

After a few weeks of basic training , we were allowed a long weekend leave, I went home to Bristol, in uniform, which was great as Mum and Dad was so proud of me. As soon as I arrived home I wanted to show myself off in my uniform as a Guardsman and went dancing.
I travelled by bus on my way to the dance held at a large Ballroom on the Downs named The Glen, and was standing on the footplate. As we drew up at a bus stop further along the route I noticed Sue, an ex-girlfriend of mine standing with a boy. 'Hey, Wow' I thought, called her name and jumped off the bus. 'How are you?' I asked, and then in my excitement remembered how things were with her, some few months earlier when she caused me so many problems.

Because of her, there'd been many fights in the past, plus I'd caught her cheating on numerous occasions, which tore me up inside, but foolishly kept having her back.
It's strange how love affects you when you're young, and despite this, this was the girl I was running away from, and ultimately why I joined the army.
She still looked stunning and commented on how smart I looked in my uniform and chatted a while as her boyfriend looked on, undoubtedly feeling somewhat uncomfortable. She then suggested we go out on the town. 'What about your boyfriend?' I asked. 'Don't worry about him' she replied, 'we can ditch him!'

That's when it all became clear. 'Yes,' I said, 'just like you used to treat me. Get lost!' Well, I never thought I'd be able to say, or do, anything like that, and as I walked away felt rather good inside at what I'd said, especially knowing how much I once loved her. I then explained to her boyfriend what she was really like, then caught the next bus to the ballroom.

At the end of my leave, I was posted to Caterham Barracks in Surrey as a proud kitted out Guardsman.

Gerald at the Guards Depot, Pirbright.

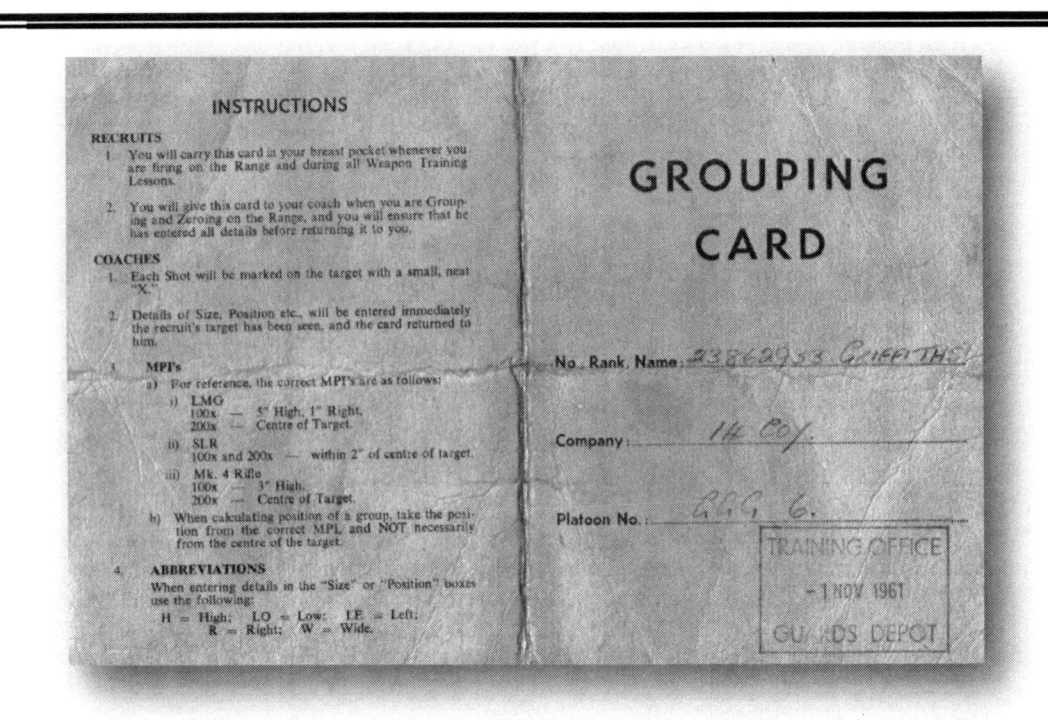

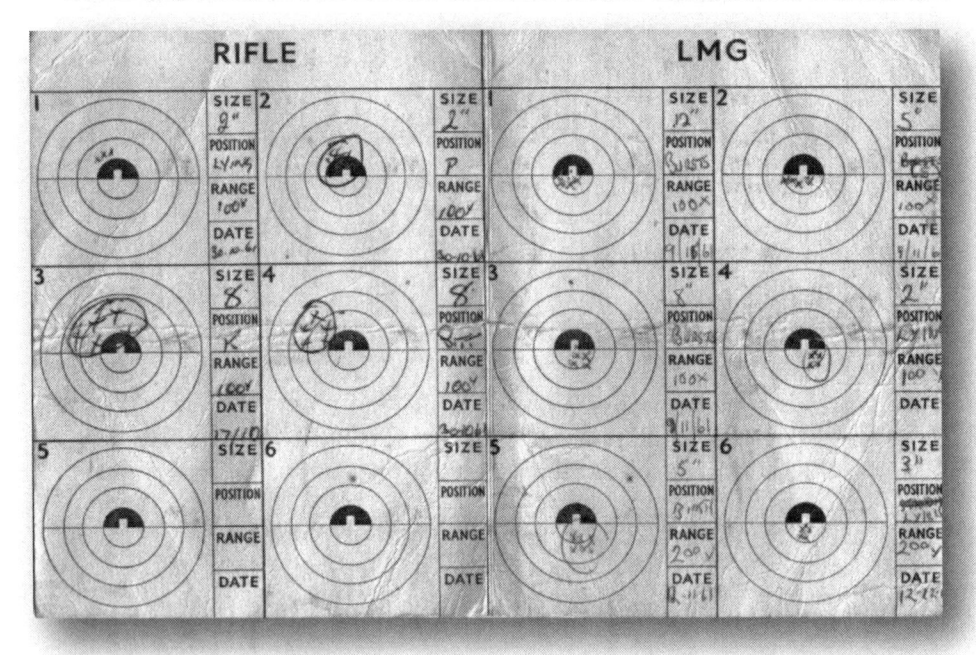

This pamphlet is the original that was signed on my ability at Pirbright 1961.

As you can see, I was a Marksman on the rifle (S.L.R), Self Loading Rifle.

The (L.M.G). Light Machine Gun, (Bren Gun).

I later became a Marksman on the (G.P.M.G.) General Purpose Machine Gun.

Most of my grouping with the Bren-Gun was very small and on centre.

S.L.R. Self Loading Rifle

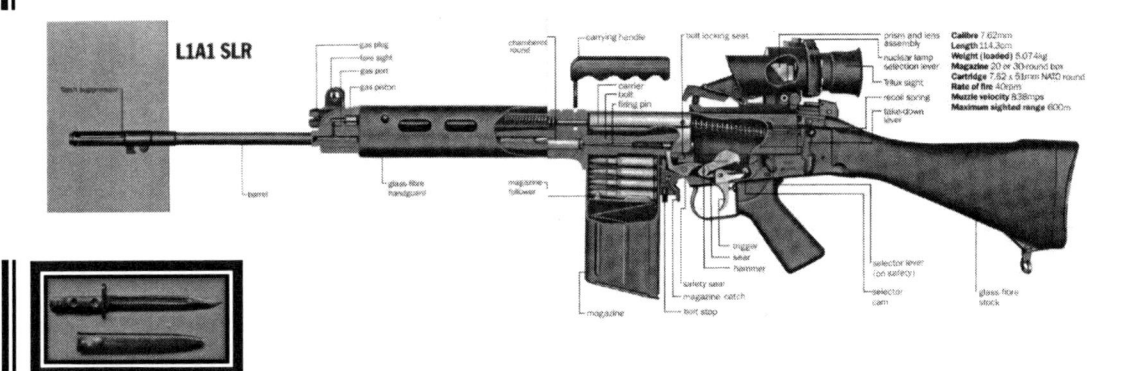

The bayonet used with the S.L.R.

The S.L.R. was my own personal weapon, which I had to keep with me at all times. It would only be put in the armoury if you were going on leave, and it had to be kept spotless as they were inspected every so often. When cleaning, it had to be stripped down to clean every part. Eventually you would be able to do this with your eyes closed, which was essential, especially if you were in the field at night. This training allowed us to do so without thinking, and without any form of light. Part of our basic training was, we had to go on the ranges at night, to shoot and also for reconition of 'sight and sound'. We had to look front and tell instructors, what we could see or here as: 'enemy front'. At night, a small sound from mess tins or even a cigarret can be seen. These smallest sights and sounds can be detected by the enemy a mile away.

As you can see in the picture at the top of this page, it can be fitted with telescopic sights, but these two pictures show general manual sights, you had to use your own adjustment and judgment, a soldier had to have greater skills, than with the weapons that came later.

Rear Sights up in picture.

7.62MM G.P.M.G. General Purpose Machine Gun.

L.M.G. Light Machine Gun, (Bren Gun).

The Browning, 30 M1919 Browning and the barrel sticking out of the turret of a Ferret Scout Car.

Adopted in 1953 for use in tanks and ferret scout cars; It featured alternate feed capability, allowing the weapon to load ammunition from either the left or the right. It had a rear charging handle and many small improvements over the 1919A4. This was the last US machine gun chambered for the 30-06 cartridge.

I have recently seen on the internet there is soon to be a small arms weapon introduced, that fires a round that will not only go round corners but into dugouts and foxholes seeking out and tracing its enemy.

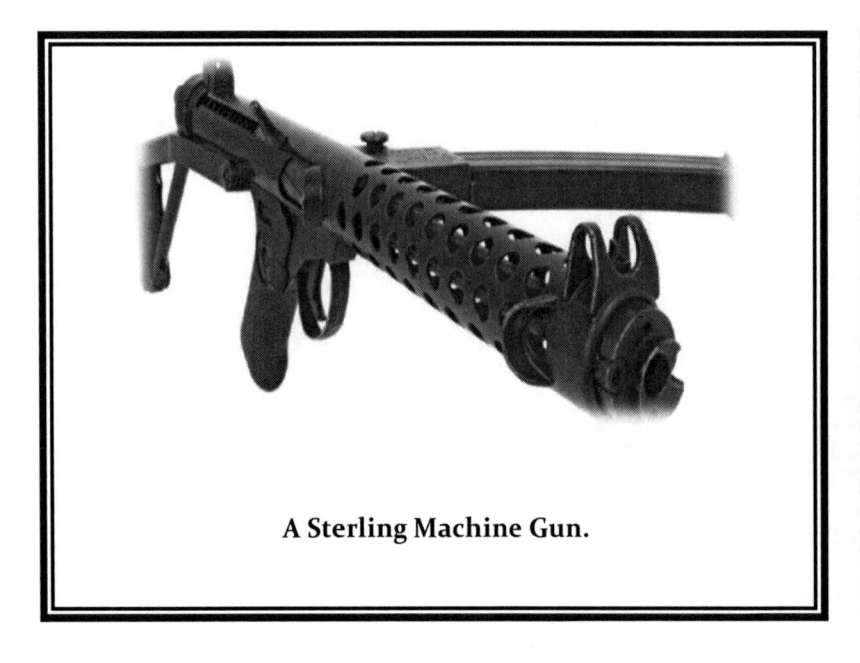

A Sterling Machine Gun.

The Sterling being a very close quarter weapon, which would be used more for jungle warfare.

Gerald at Pirbright 1961 in combat gear with Bren Gun.

One of the best weapons of it's time was the Le-Enfield. Most snippers would use this rifle for it's accuratecy, this was before the more sophisticated telescopic infa-red heat seeking sights that could see in the dark, and be able to pick up the heat from an enemy's body.

But the Le-Enfield was such a steardy weapon, you could almost chop wood with it, and it would still fire even if it was socking wet.

This Le-Enfield is being fired by my Brother Graham Griffiths, in 1953,when he served in the National Service. This was a couple of years before I enlisted, as Graham was a few years older than me. I also had two other Brothers that served their National Service, David, and Christopher. All three served before I enlisted as I missed National Service.

Photo's of my three Brothers. From left to right: Graham, David, an Christopher.

Gerald holding the (S.L.R). at the Guards Depot Pirbright.

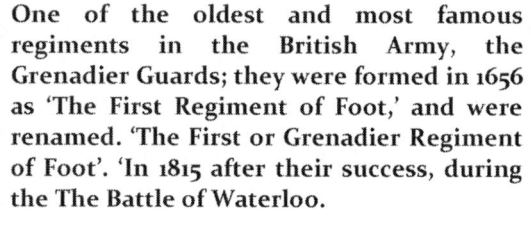

One of the oldest and most famous regiments in the British Army, the Grenadier Guards; they were formed in 1656 as 'The First Regiment of Foot,' and were renamed. 'The First or Grenadier Regiment of Foot'. 'In 1815 after their success, during the The Battle of Waterloo.

It is the senior Regiment of the Household Division and is therefore the most Senior Regiment in the British army

As a result of defence cutbacks the 2nd Battalion Grenadier Guards were placed in suspended animation in 1994, but the traditions and Colours they held, are now carried by Nijmegen Company which carries the name of the Battle Honour won by the Regiment in 1944. Nijmegen Company is currently undertaking ceremonial duties in London. The 1st Battalion is currently employed in light role.

The grouping of buttons on the tunic is a common way to distinguish between the Regiments of Foot Guards. Grenadier Guards',
Buttons are equally spaced and embossed with the Royal cipher reversed and interlaced surrounded by the Royal Garter bearing 'Honi Soit Qui Mal Y Pence', (Evil be to him who evil thinks).
Their 'Buff Belt' brass clasp also carries the Royal Cipher. Modern Grenadier Guardsmen wear a cap badge of a 'Grenade Fired Proper' with seventeen flames. This cap badge has to be cleaned, once in the morning and once in the afternoon, as it is made from brass and a tarnished Grenade is frowned upon by all in the Regiment, of the Grenadier Guards.

'Once a Grenadier, always a Grenadier!'

All though I have called my book the Autobiography of an ex Grenadier Guardsman, the title of this page says it all, for all Guardsmen remember the unique privilege of being a part of something that is recognised the whole world over. I myself am proud to have been part of this world wide stamp of the excellence of The Grenadier Guards, and still a member of the Grenadier Guards Association. The Guards of the Household Division guard: Horseguards Parade, Buckingham Palace, St James's Palace, Windsor Castle, and Her Majesty's Tower of London, and most state ceremonies, as The Sovereigns Personal Troop. These are only a few of their skills: They have fully combatant roles consisting of Armoured personal in reconnaissance, tanks and infantry skills, that cannot be surpassed by most force's of the world.

The Guards provided the Special Air Service, (S.A.S.). The Household Division supplies all the officers and men for the Guards Squadron of 22 Special Air Service Regiment. The Regiment was formed in 1941, by Colonel David Sterling, DSO, OBE, Scots Guards, and distinguished itself in numerous encounters behind enemy lines. Since then the weapons and techniques have over the years, vastly improved, but the spirit and determination required are the same as it has always been, as is the operational role of the SAS, with reconnaissance and raids by small parties into enemy held areas.

We also provided the first Battalion of the Parachute Regiments, provided entire divisions in the both World Wars and also formed a squadron of a long Range Desert Groups, (Desert Rats). We also had at one time, a Parachute Regiment which was called 'The Guards Independent Para Company', Grenadiers also fought in Aden, Borneo, and the Falklands, as well as performing peace keeping duties in Northern Ireland, where they helped counteract terrorist threat of over thirty eight years. They also helped established peace in Bosnia, Kosovo, Iraq and Afghanistan as well as many other peace keeping assignments. They have an untarnished record of outstanding service of the highest professional standard, Loyalty, Gallantry of an elite nature. These standards of character are more important today than they have been, as pride of service follows a Guardsman into his civilian life.

'So once again: 'Once a Grenadier, always a Grenadier!'

Now I had become a fully-fledged Guardsman in the Brigade of the Guards,

(The 2nd Battalion Grenadier Guards)

The Brigade of Guards

The Brigade of Guards consisted of seven Regiments. The Grenadier Guards the Coldstream Guards the Scots Guards the Irish Guards the Welsh Guards and the Life Guards, (Horseguards) which consisted of the Blues and Royals.

The five regiments of Foot Guards &

The Royal Horse Guards Division

My Pride as a Guardsman, and now an ex-Guardsman, I can look back and see how fortunate the path of my life, where fate had led me, to be able to become one of the members of the Household Brigade.

The Life Guards: The Blues & Royals and the Guards consisted of about Fifty-five hundred officers and men which had the special task of protecting the British Sovereign. Although they had this task they were also a highly trained disciplined and versatile fighting force, which has served this Country since the 17th Century.

Trooping of the Colour on the Queen's Birthday Parade, 'of which I have done four', and is one of their Military Excellences, which is choreographed to perfection and today televised around the World?

For the foreign tourist this spectacle has and remains one of fantastic fascination. I, as an Ex-Guardsman know that we all achieved this by hard work and dedication to perfection, in everything we do.

Not only keeping up our other rolls as a fighting force, 'yes we are a fighting force' which can be recognised throughout the world. So the training, combined with the ceremonial duties required to perform our tasks, can be an immense workload. This helps to pull us through as a Military self-regenerated elitism of aspic proportions to attitudes of well mannered respectful soldier of the British forces, to the devotion to the sovereignty, and to the protection of our wonderful Country, but with our discipline, loyalty, and confidence, that is induced in basic training, we achieve all this with great pride.

'I underlined we are a fighting force', as it upsets me when people generally think all we do, is stand outside Buckingham Palace, and think we are nothing but toy soldiers. Hopefully after reading this book and particularly this page they will realise that we are a fighting force and one to be reckoned with. One of the most elite fighting forces in the world. To be able to perform Ceremonial Duties one minute, and then fly into troubled spots anywhere in the world at a moment's notice, this is the mark of a true professional soldier.

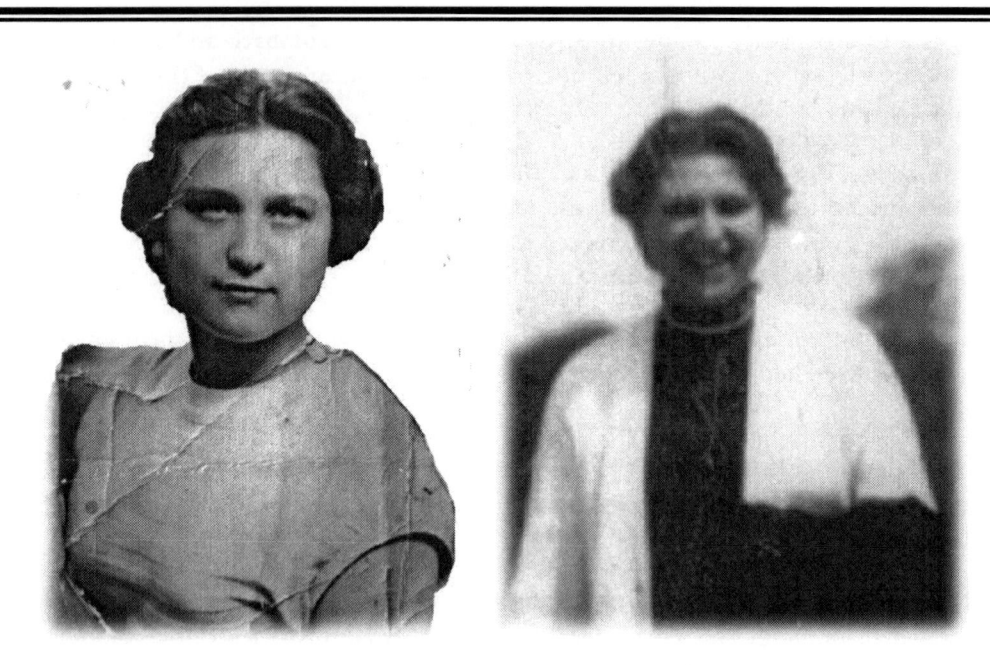

This is my sister Sheila aged fourteen in 1953 and a year later in 1954

After being in the army a few months I came home to attend my Sister's Wedding to Mr. Keith Waller, in 1961. I was dressed in my Blues uniform, Sheila looked a beautiful Bride, and the wedding took place at St Cuthbert Church, Sandypark Road, on the corner of Wick Road in Brislington Bristol.

Mum and Dad plus all my brothers and Sisters are in this picture except for Sheila.

In the foreground from left to right: The Groom Keith's brother Tony, and his sister Sue, David, Dad, Christopher, Mum, Andrew, Peter, and a friend of the family, me in uniform with hat, then Mary, the two very young ones, in the front are Annett and Julie and Angela in white brides maid. Right at the centre rear is another of Keith's brothers and his wife which is the lady in the white hat. On the extreme right is my Aunty Alice holding a bag, she was not a real aunty, but such a long close friend of Mum's in fact the story goes, 'Dad chatted her up before he know Mum', and she turned down his advance.

Dad about to give the blushing Bride, Sheila away.

FAITHFUL 5,000
They stand in silence round the Cenotaph

Bristol Evening Post.

Gerald in Bearskin as a Weeping Sentry on the left hand corner of the Cenotaph Remembrance Day Parade at Bristol
12th November 1962
For all the War Heroes who died.

Incidentally, I was Twenty one that weekend, and celebrated my birthday at home. I had a girlfriend back home at Slimbridge, in Gloucestershire who came down with my sister Mary to see me at the Bristol Cenotaph.

I was very proud to have done this, and was so moved by the ceremony. Although it was a moving tribute, it was rather hard to do as we had to stand perfectly still for almost two hours. If and when we needed a break, we had to bang, (tap) your Rifle butt on the floor, so your opposite sentry would come to attention at the same time, we then marched a few patrols and retook our positions.

When you were ready to stop patrolling , we would gave each other a signal, and both came to a halt together and went back to Rest on Arms Revere. The Rest On Arms Reversed was done from the present arms, then the rifle was reversed and the barrel end was put on your boot. Both arms, one at a time, were then outstretched to the sides then came around in an ark, and placed on the upended butt of the rifle, your arms and elbows were closed and at the same time bowed your head as in prayer, with your hands clasped around the end of the butt. In this position your Bearskin was difficult to wear, and became quite uncomfortable as it dug into your forehead, especially when your head was bowed forward.

Military Last Post.

Next time you attend a military funeral, especially one where they sound 'Last Post', I hope this story, which I found on the Internet and believe to be true, will bring out the true meaning of The Last Post.

Anyone that's served in the forces, or been standing to attention while this call was sounded, will tell you it brings a lump to the throat, and possibly a tears to the eye when this haunting melody is played. We have all heard it. But do you truly know the true story behind the call? If not, I am sure you would find its humble beginnings of interest.

Reportedly, at the beginning of 1862, and during the American Civil War, when Union Army Captain Ellicome was with his men near Harrison's Landing in Virginia, the Confederate Army was on the other side of the narrow strip of land.

During the night, Captain Ellicome heard a low moan from a soldier who was lying severely wounded on the field. Not knowing if it was a Union or Confederate Soldier, the Captain decided to risk his life and bring the stricken man back for medical attention. Crawling on his stomach through the gunfire, the Captain reached the stricken soldier and began to pull him to towards his own lines.

When the Captain finally reached his own encampment he discovered it was actually a Confederate soldier, who had since died.

Lighting a lantern the Captain caught his breath and went numb with shock, as in the dim light he saw the face of the soldier. 'It was the face of his son'.

The boy had been studying music in the south when the war broke out, and without informing his father, the boy had enlisted in the Confederate Army.

The following morning, the heartbroken father asked permission to give his son a full Military Burial, and despite his enemy status, this request was only partially granted.

The Captain had asked if he could have a group of Army Band members play a funeral dirge for his son at the funeral. This request was turned down as the soldier was a Confederate.

But, out of respect for the father, they did say they would agree to give him only one musician.

The Captain chose a bugler, and asked him to play a series of notes on a scrap of paper found in the pockets of his dead son's uniform.

This wish was granted.

This is now the haunting melody we know as The Last Post, and where it was born. Now used at all Military funerals

Please say a prayer for all those Soldiers that are away from their loved ones.

By the way I was unaware as I expect you are there are words to this Melody until this very day:

The words are:

Day is done, gone the sun, from the lakes.

From the hills, from the sky, is well.

Safely rest. God is nigh.

Fading light dims the sight.

And a star, gems the sky,

Gleaming bright, from afar

Drawing nigh, falls the night.

Thanks and praise. For our days.

Neath the sun. Neath the stars.

Neath the sky. As we go. This we know. God is nigh.

I too have felt chills while listening to the 'Last Post' but had neither seen or known there was words that accompanied this melody. I now have the deepest respect for the Melody of the Last Post, more now than I ever had.

This story will come to mind next time I find myself standing to attention at any parade, function or Funeral, remembering those that are lost or harmed while serving their country, also to those that have served and returned, as well as those presently serving in the Armed Forces.

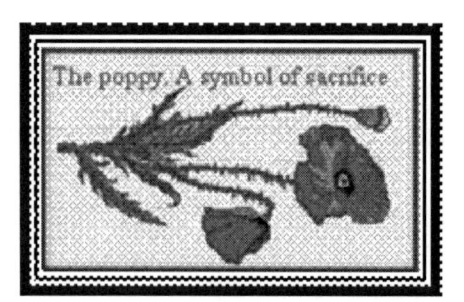

The poppy. A symbol of sacrifice

Caterham Barrack gate, by the Guard Room.

I arrived at Caterham in Surry January of 1962 and stayed there until we went to British Guyana, after the winter of 1963. I had some good times at Caterham

Inkerman Company. Barrack Room.
first on the right ground floor.

No 3 Company block, In Caterham,
where Signal Platoon were.

Caterham Barracks.

An old Humber One ton truck which is being driven down the road in Caterham Barracks past the Square on the right of the picture, and Officers-Mess on the left.

I was in the Anti Tank Platoon of No 1 Company for a short while, then went to Inkermen Company, then later moved to No 3 Company, where I attended and passed a Signal's Course. This served as an advantage to me, as when we later moved to Germany I became a Ferret Scout Car Driver in the Recognisance Platoon, as the Scout Car is equipped with a radio.

Signals Platoon, No 3 Company 1962.

The Commanding Officer inspecting the barracks.

Just passed Inkerman Company Block heading towards the N.A.A.F.I

Gerald having a rest from duty, and giving his boots a good clean.

Photo by Alan Maslin.
Gerald on Sentry in the back garden of Buckingham Palace.
Also Alan Maslin ready for duty, who became a Sgt Ferret Scout Car Commander in Germany, in the same Recognisance Platoon as myself.

The Battalion training for the Trooping of the Colour at Caterham.

In 1962, I went in the Anti-Tanks Platoon of No One Company, and attended an Anti-Tank Course at a Camp near the town of Appleby, in the North of England, near Penrith. Here, I was taught to fire the Mobat and the Wombat.

The Wombat.

Photo kind permission Stuart Davis

This is the Mobat 120mm recoilless gun, with Stuart Davis when a young L/Cpl at the controls. 1st Battalion Grenadier Guards, taken in the Gulf, (*Circa*) 1968/69

This is a Mobat 120mm recoilless gun. The Mobat & Wombat were vehicle mounted weapons. The Conbat, which I have not fired, was a converted Mobat. The difference being: instead of having a Bren Gun as spotter, it was fitted with a 0.5 mm spotting rifle.

This had a similar trajectory as the main armament unlike the Bren Gun spotter. So it was a hit on target with the spotter and 'stand by!' A similar weapon was also mounted on the Wombat.

Whilst on this course I learned that we had a new Drill Sergeant, one D/Sgt 'Bunny' Whitehead'

We heard he was an Ex Anti Tank man and when on parade took great delight in asking those wearing the Anti Tank badge what the definition of 'lead', was? So whilst on this course I took it upon myself to memorise its precise meaning, word for word from the pamphlet, and would often walk up and down the room reciting it over and over again, of which it is now embedded in my memory for ever.

Later, on returning to the Battalion, I happened to be on Guards Duty when this question was asked and even before he had finished asking, I was able to shoot the answer back and quoted:

'Lead is the amount by which the bore is directed in front of a moving target, to allow for the lateral movement of the target, during the time and flight of the projectile, *Sir!*'

He replied, '*Yes smart alec*! Then he walked off inspecting the rest of the Squad, 'I was chuffed!' These guns would have a light armament gun as well as your main armament, which at the time was a Bren Gun, 'L.M.G.' fitted with magazines filled with tracer rounds, when fired these rounds would go in a straight line to the target, so on firing the gun and seeing them hitting your target, you set off your main armament. Your main armament sights would be directed a few yards ahead of the target to allow, for a larger arc of trajectory as the main charge travelled towards the target. Each gun sights have to be calibrated for this lead.

'Which is the meaning and definition of 'Lead'?

Two 120 mm L2 Bat H.E.S.H. L19A3 Rounds. The name, H.E.S.H, stands for: High Explosive Squash Head. They are named thus, as when the explosive round exit's the gun, not only was it full of explosives, but the explosives are sealed in a fine soft wax, so when it landed on the target at whatever angle, it would not ricochet off as it hit, it would squash against the target and explode inwards, and molten metal would go spinning around inside. Incidentally even if you missed the target by ten to twenty yards, it would still give the crew a concussion.

I found the above two cases in a Second Hand Junk Shop and used them as umbrella stands. Whilst in the field on this Course, the Instructor would ask you questions about parts of the gun, and if you could not answer, would lift two of these rounds onto your shoulders, and make you run across the field to a tree some distance away at the top of a hill, (around 400 yards), go round this tree and back, and on more than one occasions found myself doing just that. When you returned he would ask the same question, for those that could still not remember, it was up the hill again! So, by the time you returned a second time, you most certainly would know the answer.

**Home on leave at Slimbridge, in 1963 with my Baby sister Angela.
I Built this Snowman for her.**

This winter was so severe I could hardly get down the side street to our house.

During the winter of 1963, and whilst serving with Inkerman Company, there was an epidemic of influenza. Feeling unwell I reported to the Sick Bay, where the medics took my temperature and bedded me down. I asked the Sergeant, who was usually bad tempered and grumpy, if I should fetch my bedding, who surprised me by saying, 'don't worry Griffiths, we will get it!' Then took me to the Barrack Room and instructed me to rest while he collected my bedding! I had never known him be nice before! This barrack room was set up for all those that were going down with this sickness. Later when I had recovered, I understood why he had been so nice, and was because my temperature was so high and I could have died! On top of the Influenza, I had Pneumonia Bronchitis!' I believe the Sergeants name was Steve Horton.

We were also on manoeuvres near Guilford during that long cold winter, and remember resting my feet a little too close to the camp fire, and although my boots were near the flames, was unable to feel any heat. I then smelled burning, and without realising, found my boots were almost on fire. I also remember we were sleeping rough in the open air, and having removed my boots prior to climbing into my Sleeping bag, placed them under my head to act as a pillow. However during the night they moved, and became exposed to the elements, and when I attempted to put them on in the morning they were as stiff as glass! I literally had to thaw them out by the fire before I could do anything with them.

There was also another incident involving an Officer and men that went out on patrol late at night. The snow was so bad it was possible to be walking six feet above ground level on a crust of ice that was on top of a layer of snow.

Without knowing the Officer led them across what he thought was a field, only to find out it was a lake when one of them fell through. I believe the person involved was Guardsman Alan 'Mush' Goddard, who told me that he thought his time was up! luckily, they were able to pull him back onto the thick layer of ice, but by the time they returned to camp his clothing was rock solid and could have stood up by themselves. He was shivering through and through and so cold, they returned him back to Barracks.

Not long after that incident, the manoeuvres were cancelled, and everyone returned to Barracks. We were told not to go near the fires for a while and let ourselves thaw out naturally. One of the guardsmen did not listen to what was said, and not knowing he had frostbite, placed his feet by the fire, and he lost his toes when Gangrene set in. I do believe there was a court inquiry over all this, as some of our equipment was inadequate.

This is a message from Mr Goddard.
From Alan Goddard, same subject.

I can confirm it was me that fell into the water all those years ago but I did not go back to Barracks and the two people who were on that patrol with me were 2nd Lt Rollo and L/Sgt Des Hart. I can remember the bloke losing some of his toes and was not because he was sat to near the fire but because he jumped into a hot bath before he was thawed out.

I have Quoted this to Alan Goddard: I distinctly remembered him putting his feet by the fire as soon as he got into barracks, and told him not to do that, and remember him saying, 'fuck off, I'm cold, so it was most likely a combination of the two, and of course, probably more so by having a hot bath.

So as you can see after all these years, what with computers and the technology we have today, we are able to stay in contact, or find out what has happened to everyone since leaving the forces, or information. This was through the thanks to Ex-Grenadier Guardsman, James White as he runs a Newsletter on the Internet called, 'Grenadiers Reunited', where old comrades can keep in touch. James gives his time freely to do this, 'thanks to James!'

After learning all about Arctic Combat, we were then flown to British Guyana for Tropical Warfare. Thanks to the government's inane ability, this is why British Forces have to be the best in the World. They can adapt and acclimatise very quickly to any place in the World.

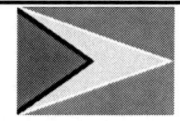

Chapter (5)

In 1963 we were then posted to British Guiana. Guiana is a country of extraordinary natural beauty, the country is situated on the northern coast of South America. This in turn is bordered to the west by Venezuela to the east by Suriname to the south and southwest by Brazil. When Guiana received its independence the spelling of Guiana change to GUYANA

Guyana is an Amerindian word which means 'Land of Many Waters', several rivers including the Demerara, the Essequibo, the Berbice, and flow from the south to north. The magnificent Kaiteur Falls, the world's highest single-drop waterfall is located on the Poaro River.

The climate is tropical with two rainy season, May to August and November to January. Guyana has one of the largest Rainforests in South America with a wide diversity of wildlife.

The population is approximately 0.77 million and the capitol Georgetown is the largest city. The majority of the population are of East Indian descent, and is the only country in South America where English is the official language. Culturally Guyana is accepted as a Caribbean Nation.

In the 17th century, Guyana was originally a Dutch Colony, and by 1815, it had become a British possession. Guyana achieved its independence from the United Kingdom in 1966. In 1992, Cheddi Jagan was elected president, and was deemed to be the first free and fair election since independence.

This picture is of the Kaieteur Waterfall, and map.

I have seen this close up, the scenery is awesome, and the noise deafening. It is said there are millions of pounds worth of diamonds at the bottom of these falls? But, because of the force of water cascading down, are unreachable. It is also the highest fall of water in the world.

To put things into perspective: Kaieteur Falls is around five times higher than the well known Niagara Falls, and is one of the most spectacular waterfalls in the world. It has a free fall height of over 700 feet, and it is one of the few places in the world where endangered species are easily observed. The specially designed on-site nature walk places you face-to-face with the many and varied exotic plant and animal species.

Kaieteur Waterfalls Guyana.

Kaieteur can be admired close up, or filmed from varying distances as well as from numerous angles. Aerial views of the falls are truly spectacular. Kaieteur National Park is situated on the Guiana Shield, a plateau that is one of the world's oldest and remotest geological formations. The entire Kaieteur National Park is located within one of the largest and most bio diverse rainforests in the world. The Falls are accessible by both land and air. By air, it is an hour's flight from Georgetown, the Capital of Guyana.

By land there is a popular adventurous wilderness trek, that requires three to four days to complete, which is how I got there, which is a story all by its self, which I hope to tell in the future.

All Photos of Kaieteur Falls are credited to Guyana news and information. www.guyana.org

Kaieteur Waterfalls Guyana.

Guyana is known as the land of many waters

Camp Street 10th February 1964.
I can remember walking down this very road, and in the distant noticed a woman crouched down. By the time I reached her, she had, had a baby right there in the street! She picked it up and carried on walking. In Tommy Cooper's own words, just like that! 'Amazing!'

Photos credited to www.guyana.org

This is Part of Georgetown from the Air.
The Atlantic Ocean in the back ground, and alongside the Demerara River.

During my time in Guyana I was part of the Inkerman Company.
There were many incidents in and around the capital of Georgetown. Some of these were downright dangerous, and prior to the 2nd battalion arriving there, there was a state of Active Emergency imposed, and can remember when we first arrived having to engage with armed, crowds. Most had knives' and machetes, the machetes being the tool of their trade, as Sugar Cane Cutters.
One of the main reason the British Forces were in Guyana was to keep the opposing factions apart, which was similar to the troubles in Northern Ireland, and was all to do with the Vote, and voting for the Governing Body.

Another day, another Riot.
On a military level, one particular day we were called out to attend a riot outside a sugar plantation and as we arrived in our three ton trucks, formed ourselves into the now familiar riot formation square, with marksmen in the front rank. As the crowd was extremely aggressive, we immediately took a firm stance with weapons at the ready.
The Riot Square or Formation is where all soldiers are facing outwards with the exception of those men at each corner, who face at an angle. Inside the square is a small group comprising of an officer, Sergeant and two or three other ranks. In this instance, the officer was the Second Lieutenant Master of Rollo and the Sergeant was Sgt Talkington, Those in the centre held up a warning sign, usually in two languages stating: Disperse, or we will open fire! While the officer using a loud hailer also, warned the crowd to disperse or we would open fire.

I was in the front rank with the Marksmen, and this forward rank was numbered from one to ten, with numbers distributed unevenly, so that in the event of a shot being fired no one would know who was responsible. To be called out for Riot Duty would first depend on how large the crowd was, and an assessment would be needed for the numbers of soldiers to make this response.

The angry crowd was not dispersing, so the officer ordered: 'Front rank ready!' All soldiers in the front rank would take the firing position. The officer then ordered, 'Number four will fire!' 'My God I thought, 'that's me!' The officer then assesses and describes the person he thinks is the main agitator ringleader, plus where he is in the crowd. All front-rank will call, *'seen!'* to acknowledge they know which the target is, but only the designated numbered person will fire. As I have said this was me, my trigger finger had taken up the slack and had him in my sights awaiting the order to fire. I knew I was capable of doing the job, and what I had been trained to do, and would fire on the word of command. As I said the slack was off the trigger and I was waiting for the order to fire. Then as quickly as everything had happen, when they realised we meant business the crowd started to disperse, we had the order to stand down and unload, Looking back as I write this, and now that I am older, I'm so glad I did not have to shoot him.

The S.L.R. fires a seven point six two millimetre (7.62mm) round and was the rifle I had, which if I had to fire, would probably had gone right through the target, out the other side, and hit and gone through at least two or three or more other people behind him. Knowing that, I would have that on my conscience for the rest of my life.

Well, in a reasonable short time things began to settle down in the country, and calm was restored. We were more often deployed at sugar plantations, plus their estates, as well as providing Platoons at various locations throughout the areas. The state of emergency eventually lifted, and we were able to go on adventurous and various exercises into the interior, most of the time with live ammunition. While looking back on these States of Emergencies and episodes, and thinking of my family back home and would I get home in one piece, everything was happening so fast, my life was becoming such a blur, and was glad when things settled down.
I remember we, that is a small Platoon of about eight or nine of us with an officer in charge, plus two guides' had gone right into the interior by two small dugout rafts, which was pulled along by a horse on the riverbank trailing a long rope. Incidentally I was allowed to ride this horse as I could ride before I went in the forces. God was my ass sore!

We were allowed to stay in a shack that belonged to a large farm estate, which herded wild buffalo. After we settle in, the officer allowed four of us to go down river on our own in a Dugout Canoe. The actual river was flooded and was quite wide as it was in the rainy season. We had gone a few miles and could see a rundown shack in the distance, which looked old and derelict and and as if no one was there. One of my mate's I think it was, 'Ben Gun' his proper name being Erick Gun, who had been given this nickname from the character in the novel 'Treasure Island'. He laid down a challenge by saying 'I bet you can't hit that shack from here?' I replied 'No, there may be someone there', which he answered 'no you can see its empty and run down.

Taking up the challenge, I took a prone position in the front of the boat and fired off two or three rounds. Remember what I said earlier in my writing. 'The velocity of the 7.62 rounds is capable of passing through around ten people? Well we kept rowing for around a mile or so and eventually reached the shack. As we climbed out of the dugout onto the bank, we could see the shack was indeed rundown and derelict, but we were gobsmacked when an old woman walked out of the shack. I then I realised how stupid I'd been to have listened to my mates, as one of my rounds had gone right through her shack and out the other side! Lucky for me, and more luck for her, it did not hit her, and she was oblivious of the bullet going through her shack. She must have been stone deaf,' as it would have made one hell of a loud 'crack' as it passed through, and at the time her man was out fishing.

Whilst in Guyana, I had many encounters with various snakes from, Anaconda's to Rattles Snake's. Here are some of my stories. My first encounter was when I was stationed at the Diamond Sugar Plantation, which was on the route to the Airport. This had Rainforest on either side of the road and was not that far from Georgetown. There was an Anaconda or Boa-Constrictor, which had been crossing the road, when its tail was run over by a car. We caught it with the help of a nearby local who cooked it and myself and some of my mate's had some. I was quite surprised at how nice it tasted, it was just like pork steaks. It was so large around ten feet in all, and would have fed our entire Platoon! It certainly fed his family, and that's how some of the people out there would live, 'by hunting'.

This one got to be about twenty odd feet.

Alan Fowler on the Berbice going to Takama.

Alan Maslin with 'Big' Ben Smith and Mick Starky on the Berbice river.

For me to give you some idea of how large these snakes can grow: When visiting a Zoo in Georgetown. I noticed a Boa 'Constrictor in a cage, which was only wire mesh, and asked the Keeper how many snakes were in the cage, as I thought there were around nine or ten. He said only one, I could hardly believe it as it was everywhere, up and over the tree along the ground, back up the trees and down onto the floor again. It was huge!

The Anaconda lives in the swamps and rivers of the rainforest.
They can climb trees and swim very quickly, and kill their prey by constricting or squeezing it. The python holds the world's record for the length of any snake, with the longest ever measuring 33 feet. Even though the longest python is longer than the record-holding Anaconda, the girth of an Anaconda is far larger. Anacondas in the jungles of South America can grow as large in width as a grown man.

Anaconda.

Later on in the months, we travelled by boat up the Berbice River, then on into the interior to a place called Takama, we were on the open Savona at this camp. It was in really wild country, which was only about two miles from the Equator. The whole of Inkerman Company were on Spearhead Patrol, and during these manoeuvres firing live ammunition. I was on the right flank of the Spearhead as Bren Gunner, and preferred walking behind someone, following in their tracks through the long grass, in the hope they would have scared off any snakes. But this time, being on extreme right flank, there was no one ahead of me!

I think I must have a phobia about them. They were in great abundance in this part of the country, mostly Diamondback Rattlesnakes', (*Crotalus Adamanteus*). These could grow to around five or six feet long, and can tell how old they are by the amount of rings on their rattles. I was also told that if you were too close to them, they would start to rattle their tail. But, when they were about to strike, their rattle would stop, as they can't strike unless their tail is on the ground. Anyway as I was walking, instead of searching for the enemy, I was watching the ground looking for snakes!

So, if you imagine, there I am looking on the ground when I heard, *'Get down Griffiths, get down!* I looked up as I was still walking and noticed everyone had vanished into the long grass. I then realised the enemy must be to my front. I then went to throw myself down, and to my horror found a large Rattlesnake between my feet that had obviously been asleep in the Noonday sun, and had not heard my approach. You can imagine how, in cartoon's, when a startled character jumps in the air with his feet still spinning, and then shooting off with a '(*pitooooooowwww*)', without touching the ground? That was me! Everyone was shouting. *Get down, get down!* But I took no notice shouting, 'Fxxx-off! There's a ruddy snake here!

If this was for real and been fighting proper enemy I would probably have been dead by then! Anyway, after that I got myself down and engaged the targets that were seen, and then performed a right flanking manoeuvre to engage the enemy. While point was firing live ammunition, we obviously stopped firing when the remainder with Bayonets fixed performed the charge. Being the Bren Gunner, I was giving cover fire, and directed my shots at targets, which had been erected weeks in advance in preparation for these Manoeuvre's. These were in a large clump of trees, around four or five hundred yards to our front, and shot them up rather well! When we had finished, we stopped for a smoke break, and received a right telling off from my superior's, for not obeying orders! 'But, was not, thank God, put on a charge! During this smoke break we went back to where I'd seen the snake, where one of my mates, Dave Hennessey, killed it, then our Guide cooked it later that day. After the Guide had skinned the snake he dried the skin and gave it to me as a souvenir. This I brought back home and kept for years, until my wife June threw it away without my knowledge. It would appear she didn't like it.

During that same smoke-break, I looked at Dave and noticed a large Scorpion on his neck, which must have dropped from one of the tree's we'd recently shot up, I told him not to move and reaching over, carefully swiped it off. Old Dave Hennessy always appeared to be involved with Snakes, Tarantulas, Scorpion, or reptiles of one form or another, which seem to be attracted to him.

Two Diamondback Rattlesnake.

While we were staying in the open campsite at Takama, Savona Plains, and living in outbuildings with no windows or doors. I had further encounters with snakes, while we were outside the cookhouse in the queue for our evening dinner and dusk was falling. On the corner by the cookhouse wall, were some old pototoe sacks that had been placed, where we were standing. After dinner, I then went on guard patroling around the camp plus all the buildings.

As I passed these potatoe sacks I saw some movement, and using the barrel of my Rifle carefully lifted these sacks and found a Diamondback Rattlesnake with a clutch of young below them. To think, only an hour or so earlier we were all standing right there oblivous of the fact the snakes was mere inches away, 'it doesn't bear thinking about what could have happened!'

Discribing the huts we lived in. These had a long low wall approximately four foot high around the base and above that, from the top of the wall to the roof wooden uprights a couple of yards apart, with no windows, while the doorways was just wide open gaps in the wall. One particular night I awoke at reveille and started to get out of my bed, which were small camp beds around a foot of the ground, while doing this, I looked across to one of my mates, he was just about to get out of bed himself when I noticed a Diamondback under his bed. I quickly shouted to him, to stay where he was, and he had to climb out of bed onto the wall. Then useing a long stick we carefully got rid of the thing.

The most frieghtening encounter happened one particular night, when I had to get up to go to the latrines. When doing this, we had to take a torch, and follow a long track through well worn grass, which was some way off. These Latrine were a cluster of small huts, covering a series of holes over which crude boxs with holes and toiletseats had been placed on the top, these were known as: 'thunder box's!. Anyway back to my story, The light from the torch could hardly reach the ground, and as I made my way forward, suddenly I heared a (*Rattle*), I (*Fxxx'ing*) froze, perfectly still for what seemed a lifetime, as I then slowly began shinning my useless torch in vain, hoping of find where it was. I still could not find it. I knew the (*Rattle*) was very close, I remembered what I was told, they say that if he's rattling he's not in the air to strike. But suddenly the '*Rattle stopped*! That was when I panicked and ran like Hell! 'Maybe that's what saved me? Whatever it was, I never went to the toilet that night.

For us to wash and shave we had to go down to this stream, it was a fast moving stream at times, specialy when we had rain, and was around half a mile away, down in a gully. This stream was right on the age of the interior which was quite dense and thick and was a good cover for most animals which would come down to drink. These included Deers, Pigs, and a host of others, but not the morning I was there!

That paricular morning I had just arrived and was the one of the first one's there, and as I entered the clearing managed to startle a large Black Panther drinking from the stream! There's not that many around, 'but this shows they certainly were around! Lucky for me he seemed more afraid of me than I was of him. 'Thank God' I was not his dinner that day, perhaps he was not hungry as he bounded away into the Jungle leaving me quaking in my boots.

We often sat in this stream to cool off, but one day I went futher up where it was deeper, and the water came up to my neck. While there, blistfully enjoying the cool water, I was horrified as a huge Anoconda gracefully swam past, ('floating by') with the fast flowing current. My God, I've had some lucky escapes?

Ha, Ha! Had you there!

They're not real, they're stuffed, and for sale. I'm not that daft to put my hand that close to a real one.

Gerald crossing the Demerara River on the ferry.

Four major rivers cross the Guyana coastal plain from west to east the Essequibo, the Demerara, the Berbice, and the Courentyne.
The Demerara flows in eastern Guyana and its source is found in the Maccari Mountains. It flows north for 230 miles and enter the Atlantic Ocean at Georgetown. The Demerara is navigable for ocean-going vessels for approximately 60 miles upriver from the mouth to the bauxite town of Linden, formerly known as Mackenzie.

Demerara Harbour Bridge Georgetown. This river gave the name to the county of Demerara wherein Georgetown is situated, and after which, Demerara Sugar, Demerara Rum, and Demerara Windows, are named.

The Berbice River in eastern Guyana, is approximately 300 miles long, and flows northward to the Atlantic. The Berbice is navigable for up to 175 miles from the entrance. Crab Island is located at the mouth of the Berbice River. The town of New Amsterdam which is 62 miles west of Georgetown, is located on the river's eastern bank, around four miles inside the river's estuary.

Here's another story. If I remember correctly, we were staying on a Sugar Plantation and had been given permission to go Alligator hunting at night. Our group consisted of, Sergeant Talkington, Sergeant Gearing, our driver and myself. We were able to find the Alligators as the lights of the vehicle, reflected in their eyes. I managed to shoot an Alligator, or it may have been a Crocodile that was on the track to our front and we all helped to lift in it onto the canopy of our Land Rover to take back to camp.

On our way back to Camp, both Sgt Gearing and myself were leaning out of the vehicle with the canopy behind us. The going being so bumpy, I decided to lift myself up and sit on the canopy next to the Alligator. We thought it was dead, which it wasn't! As I sat on the canopy it came around and bit me on the backside, leaving me with six or seven painful teeth marks embedded in my skin! When we arrived back to camp I had to report to the M.O for a tetanus injection, and luckily had no lasting effects. Incidentally I was recently speaking to Sergeant Gearing on the telephone and discussing this incident, which he still remembers after all these years. **Facts about this animal,** we think it may have been the Crocodile (*Yacare*)

The yacare is similar in appearance to *Caiman Crocodilus*, and reaches a total length of 2.5 to 3 m. Like the common Caiman, its scales have well-developed osteoderms. The less ossified flanks are used in the skin trade. The teeth are more visible than in the common caiman, whereby certain large teeth in the lower jaw may protrude through the top surface of the upper jaw. Female Yacares build mound nests, into which 21 to 38 eggs are usually laid, which they guard during incubation.

Female Crocodile, (Yacare)

Gerald in out of bounds Aeria in Georgetown.

Another great story occurred when we did a tour of Bank's Brewery in Georgetown. After the tour, we were taken to a room at the top of the building where we could drink as much as we liked! Needless to say by the time we left I was rather drunk, and returned to barracks in the back of a three ton truck, with my head over the side being sick!

Anyway, later that day, it being a weekend, I went off to meet Jeanette a girl I was courting, and later that night was walking her home. She lived just of the Cemetery Road in Kitty Village, which to get there we had to skirt the Dockland's; this was not only a pretty rough area, it was also an Out of Bounds Area for Armed Forces, and if caught would be on a charge. Most of the dockers' were big guys and pretty rough as well, and as we came to a corner where they hung out, there must have been ten or twelve of them. Ignoring this we walked on, but as we passed by they began calling out bad names like: 'Look at the limey Scunt with his Wobin!' You can see what the first word means, while Wobin means Whore, or Prostitute! Well with all the drink inside me and little fear, I told the girl wait while I went back to confront them. She tried to stop me. But I was determined to have words about what they'd said, and stormed up to them saying, 'if any of you Fxxx-ing Bastards want trouble you can have it!' Maybe because I did it with confidence, especially after all the drink I'd had, they looked up and said, 'Sorry man'. (Mon) 'We were just having fun.' It felt rather good as I walked away, and added, 'just you watch yourselves next time!'

Well, a couple of days later, I found myself passing this same corner on my way to see her again, only this time, stone cold sober! As I reached the corner where they hung out, I could see around a dozen or so and thought, 'Oh No!' and was Shitting Bricks, knowing if they said anything again I'd have to show no fear and back it up, after all I was a British Soldier! 'Oh well, here goes' I thought and tried to get a nice swagger going as I walked past. I was hoping they'd not say something, but knew deep down they would, and with a sigh of relief, they just said 'Goodnight Soldier!' I did learn later, that a couple of big tough guys who were absent without leave from the Black-Watch had caused havoc in this area with their drinking and fighting and it did take a whole Platoon to arrest them. So, by this, the British Soldier had something of a reputation, especially in this area, and this is most likely what actually saved me?

On a night-time expedition, we were out in the Land Rover and hit a huge Owl. We got out of the cab, picked it up, and were taking it back to camp. There was three of us in the cab and placed the Owl on the floor. But as we drove along it regained conscious and started flapping around in the cab, we ended up scratched, and clawed, and somehow managed to get the door open where it flew off into the night. That's the last time we would do something like this.

Gerald ready to go out on the town in Georgetown & on the way into town on a three tonner with two sergeants. Me turning my head, then L/Sgt Ron Goldsmith, and L/Sgt Tony Walmsley accompanying me from the Diamond Plantation.

During my time in British Guiana or Guyana, as it's now called, I practised Chinese Boxing with a Doctor and his family, which they asked me not to mention and was sworn to secrecy; 'Oops sorry!' This had a great impact on my life as I went on to practice Martial Arts and still do so, to this present day.

Oh; I must tell you this one. We were 14 Company of the Inkerman Company, and in a Barrack Room, on the seafront of Georgetown, when a Dolby Women, someone that does laundry for payment, came up to me, with a piece of paper in her hand. As she both liked and trusted me. She said 'Gerry, 'Gerry can you help me mon, (man) these solders owe me money?' I took the paper she was waving, which was a list of names of those Soldiers owing her money. Here I should point out she could neither read nor write, and the solders had written their own names. On looking at the names I saw and quote: Elvis Presley 1935, Battle of Hastings 1066, US President 1963, and so on, all the names and numbers were to do with famous people, and were fictitious nothing to do with the solders that owed her money, and of course, as she could not read, she foolishly trusted them.

The poor old women would only be able to live on the money she earned by cleaning clothes and selling fruit outside the gates of the Barracks. I took the note to the Company Sergeant Major, and from this he place the entire company on the gate, which meant no solder was allowed to leave Barracks until this lady had been paid. Being a weekend, they were all looking forward to going out on the town. Later that same day the old women came running up to me, her hands full of money, 'Gerry, Gerry look mon, all this money.' What had happened was, every man, including those not owing her money, had chipped in just so they were able to go out and visit their favourite local Alehouses. That day, the old women received more money than she would have received for working all year! For her it would have been like winning a Million on the Lottery, and now considered herself quite rich.

For a couple of months we were going to be stationed at a place near the town of 'New Amsterdam', which was another large town in Guyana, but we were a few mile out in the rural outskirts around half hour's drive away and stationed at the Mackenzie Sugar Plantation. This was near the coast, which was around half a mile down the road an easy walk from the plantation.

We had travelled there on a slow moving the train, which to us seemed to be going at a steady running pace, while to one side of the track were Banana Plantations. As I was always running to keep fit, I commentated to the lads, 'I could run faster than the train!'

One of the lads said, 'I'll bet you a packet of fags, you can't jump of the train run over to the Plantation, pick some bananas and get back on again!' This was a bit risky, but I took them up on their challenge. I jumped off the train ran like Hell! All the lads where cheering and shouting, as I picked a couple of banana's and began making my way back. Whether it was me not running fast enough, or the train picking up speed I'll never know, but running alongside the train trying to get back on proved more difficult than I thought and a great deal harder to do! I did manage to get back on but only just, and that being on the last but one carriage. These carriages had no windows, just an open foot plate and stairs leading up, which I just managed to climb. The train shown in this photo is not the actual one, I took this photo in America, and it would have been around the same size.

We started to settle into this Sugar Plantation; and during this Peace Keeping Role was really there for the benefit of the local population as a show of force. One night, some of the lads, decided to go down to what we in England would call, 'The Pub', which was basically a shack where everyone gathered to have a drink. That night, there were quite a few people inside, mostly Cane Cutters on their way home from work and many of them still had their knives and machetes with them. The N.A.F.F.I. came wherever we went, and this time was no different, and as they sold it quite cheaply many of the lads nipped in and purchased a bottle of Demerara Rum prior to proceeding to, 'the pub'.

As the evening wore on, things started to get a little heated. I thought it best to leave, and said to one of my mates, 'Come on, and let's go!' But he refused to listen! I then decided that, as it looked as though there was going to be trouble, it would be best to go back and get help. As I was leaving, one of my mates named Joe Bain came up and said, 'Don't go Gerry, there's going to be a punch up!' I replied. 'Are you stupid or what? They've got knives and Machetes and we've got nothing!' As I hadn't opened my bottle, he then remarked. 'You're only going because you don't want to share your bottle of rum!' I then broke the seal, pulled out the cork, placed it to my lips and took a long large swig of Rum. God, as it went down it was really warming! I then handed him the bottle, told him to keep it, and left!
The road back to base was really a track with three ruts, the centre one being where our three ton truck's differential gearbox scraped a line in the ground, and I had only got around half the way back to base when the large swig of rum I had, overcame me and started to feel drunk. That's all I remember until waking up under a shower back at base! Apparently, two Cane Cutters from the Plantation had found me slumped in one of the ruts and lifted me out and placed me on the side of the track, which was lucky for me, for as they just lifted me of the track, one of our three ton trucks came down and they wouldn't have seen me laying in the long grass, and would have run over me! I was so lucky!
'As for the lads? They were collected by this same three ton truck, taken back to base and given a severe reprimand! I understand someone must have telephoned the base before I could have got there.

Not long after this incident, the Battalion moved back to England.

Chapter (6)

Two different parts of the same dinner queue at Caterham.
Do any of you Grenadiers recognise anyone? Or are you in it?

We came home from Guyana on the 21st of March 1964 And back to Caterham.

Junior Guards Company.

During the year of circa 1964 I spent much of my time at the Guards Training Depot, where all the Guards Divisions are trained and became a Trained Soldier Instructor in the Junior Guardsman's Company. When the entire Junior Guardsmen's Company went on block leave, I stayed on the rear party looking after the barracks.

During this time, a full Sergeant from the Irish Guards asked me to look after his dog. The dog was good and I looked after him well, until I went around checking all the doors making sure everything was secure. However, there was a barrack room door that was open, and I went in to check everything was OK. I then came back out, locking the door, and carried on checking the remainder of the Barracks. I remember calling the dog, but he didn't come, and searched the entire barracks and still couldn't find him. I had looked everywhere! But as it was late, had to abandon my search and go to bed.

The following morning, I resumed my search, but still could not find him; I looked everywhere with no success. Later that day, I thought I had better check all the barrack rooms were secure, and went around checking all the doors.

When I arrived at the door of the Barrack Room I'd earlier found unlocked, I heard a whimpering sound and unlocked the door and found the dog, which was rather pleased to see me, but no more than I was to see him! I then fed and watered the poor thing, which was so hungry it wolfed the lot down in one go.

I was so relieved to have found him, and can't to this day understand why I'd not thought of looking for him there in the first place. The Barrack Room was a mess! Dog faeces were everywhere; he had managed to pull some of the curtains down, and had been on most of the beds.
I had to clean everything, which was a small price for me to pay, rather than someone else finding him and was on the verge of contacting the Police, as well as informing the Irish Guards Sergeant, to tell him I had lost his dog. This is the first time I've related this story.

Junior Guards Company Staff. I am fifth from the left rear rank of photo.

There were five Regiments in the Junior Guardsman's Company: the Grenadier guards, Coldstream, Guards, Scots Guards, Irish Guards and the Welsh Guards.

This is a photo of part of the Junior Guards Company. I am the six's person from the right, front rank. Directly behind is Denis Randle R.I.P. our Sergeant Major's son, a young David Higgs, top rank left is Richard Nettleton. This is the Grenadier's section of the photo as the rest of it was too long for this book.

Whilst with the Junior Guardsman's Company we went to the Isle of Wight for Summer Camp and whilst there I learned to water ski. At the time the Company Commander, Major Phillipson was towing me in his speedboat somewhere out in the Solent and I was doing quite well, until he cut his engine and I sank in the water. When he came over I lifted the ski's into the boat, but the Major would not let me on board and had to swim back, something like a mile and a half back through dangerous water and shipping lanes. When I finally managed to swim back and stagger ashore, the Officer informed me I'd been in no danger as he'd been circling me at a distance and knowing there were no large liners around, and had been perfectly safe. These words did not help at all! I was quite panicky swimming in the strong currents. I was a strong swimmer as were my brothers as we were swimming all the time when we were young. Both Graham and David were good Water Polo Swimmers, especially Graham Senior. This held me in good stead for this incident and felt proud to be able to swim that far.

We were billeted under canvas similar to the one seen in this photo which shows Junior L/Sgt David Higgs's.

Photo by David Higgs.

Towards the end of 1964 I returned to Caterham, then volunteered for The Guards Independant Parachute Company, and went to their base at the Guards Depot. Prior to proceeding to the Parachute Regiment, you had to completed a pre-hardner course with their Selection Unit, and because they like to have a one hundred persent pass rate, the training was exceptionaly hard! This was far harder than the actual course itself.

One of the hardest thing I had to do during this course was, 'the two minute milling! And had to fight, not box, for two minute's. The ring was made up by placing four gym benches in a square, and we had to keep punching each other without bobbing or weaveing, for the full two minutes, which felt like the longest two minutes of my life. I was knocked down twice, but the serving Para's that came to watch, and were sitting on these benches, would pull you to your feet each time and were made to carry on, until the full two minutes were up.

The course consisded, of loads of running, mostly in full Combat Kit, and were required to work as a team at all times. This was accomplished by them insisting we carry a log, some ten to twelve feet long, and had to take it everwhere, even when off duty! It even had to accompany us to the Cookhouse each and everytime we went for a meal, Breakfast Dinner and Tea, this log had to go with us, and we had to run, not walk!

We were supplied with rope slings, which would go around the log, and there would be about twelve men carrying it, six men intermitent either side.
We also trained jumping from a platforms, in readiness for the real thing when jumping from aircraft and were taught how to land and roll with both feet together. I was rather disapointed at the end of this course to find I'd not been selected, and returned to unit (R.T.U).

Part of the Assault Course at Pirbright.

I had always held a fascination for knives, and enjoyed training in the art of Bayonet Combat. However, their emphasis was on the use of this weapon and its killing aspect, and not on the art itself, which is my interest.
At the time I owned a Commando Stiletto Knife, which was not a throwing knife, so much more judgment was needed and I wanted to be good at this, and with practice, could throw the knife rather well.

In 1962, whilst on exercise on Salisbury Plain, I met the late King Hussein of Jordan, who had watched me throwing this knife and remarked on how well I'd done, then asked me to show him how it was done. I then taught him the art of Knife Throwing. In addition to this, I also heard he went on to become a Black Belt in Karate, and would like to think I had something to do with this?'

King Hussein invited me to go out to Jordan as his guest whenever I could, but was unable to take advantage of his offer and sadly, did not go.

King Hussein of Jordan was Born; 14th November 1935, and died 7th February 1999, of Hodgkin's Lymphoma.

King Hussein was a member of: the King Abdullah, believed to have been a direct descendant of the Prophet Muhammad.

The 18 year old Hussein took the throne in 1953 following the death of his Grandfather, King Abdullah. He was schooled in Egypt as well as at the British Royal Academy Sandhurst, which is where we first met.

The young Prince Hussein attended Primary School in Amman, Egypt after which he became a Student at Britain's Sandhurst. At Sandhurst, he learned Military Principles and attitudes that helped in later years with his own Arab Army, which in turn became a key to his own experiences on the Throne of Jordan.

The most important formative influence on the Prince though was his Grandfather, King Abdulla, who was his guide and tutor. From him, Hussein learned both respect for tradition, as well as his openness for change, and was known for building some stability in the middle-east.

Back at Windsor, and during the year 1965 the 2nd Battalion Grenadier Guards were calibrating the 150th anniversary of the Battle of Waterloo!

Large Marquees had been set up in the grounds of Victoria Barracks. This was to become my most memorable encounter with most of the Royal Family, including Her Majesty the Queen!
As the Royal Family was invited, I was one of those detailed to become a waiter, and during those celebrations actually waited on Her Majesty serving drinks to her table.

Princess Anne, Princess Alexandra and most of the Royal Family plus Lords and Ladies also attended this event. These celebrations went on through the night and breakfast was served the following morning. There were stunningly beautiful girls in wonderful evening gowns, as well as handsome young Officers and Gentlemen, all dancing the night away. But, I was sworn to secrecy as to what I had seen during these festivities, cannot remark on them.

That same year, 1965, as the Queen was moving residence from Buckingham Palace to Windsor, I remember being on baggage Fatigue at Windsor Castle, and was to offload all baggage from a series of three ton trucks and place them in the Queen and Duke of Edinburgh's bedrooms. During this they were both talking to us instructing, 'what went where.'
So, I can claim to have been in both the Queen, and Prince Phillip's bedrooms!

The Archway is the gateway leading to 'The Long Walk'. 　　One of the rooms of an Officer I worked for.

Mum at Windsor Castle around 1999 with a Sentry at the main gate.

Gerald, dressed in his Guards Ceremonial BearSkin and Tunic.

The Ensign is flying, so the Queen is in residence.

Photo by Royal house of Windsor

The Signal Platoon preparing to mount guard at Windsor Castle in 1965.

2nd Battalion Grenadier Guards Corps of Drums, Drum Major Metcalf changing guard at Windsor Castle winter 1965

Both photos by David Higgs

Drum Major Metcalf leading 2nd Battalion Grenadier Corps of Drums with the Guard Detachment dismounting Guard and marching back to Victoria Barracks. Winter 1965.

Photo by David Higgs.
2nd Battalion Grenadier Guards Corps of Drums, with Guard Detachment Dismounting Guard, 1965.

Photo presented by David Higgs
This is either the 1st or 2nd Battalion Grenadier Guards on Guard Dismount, Windsor Castle circa 1960.

Photo, credits to Royal house of Windsor

The 'Long Walk', Windsor.

There was a funny incident when I was on Sentry Duty at Windsor Castle, and was on the Post known as, 'The Long Walk.'
The Long Walk is an avenue of trees with a carriageway in the centre leading from Windsor Castle, and is just under three miles long. This leads to a large mound known as Snow Hill, where a Statue of George III known as, 'The Copper Horse' can be found.

I was standing at ease at my post at the top of this avenue when I noticed three or four Corgi Dogs coming out of the Castle, and one of these Corgi's was cocking its leg and urinating on my boots! I then heard voices, it was the Queen and Duke of Edinburgh taking their dogs for a walk. I then came smartly to attention and Presented Arms! But, when I stamped my feet it frightened the dog and it started barking at me.
The Queen acknowledged my salute and apologised for the dog's behaviour, then carried on with their walk.

The Long Walk was commenced by Charles II from 1680-1685 by planting a double avenue of elm trees. The central carriageway was added by Queen Anne in 1710. The original planting comprised 1,652 trees placed 30 feet apart in each direction. The width between the two inner rows was 150 feet, and overall 210 feet. It is a little less long than the original proposed three miles, it being around 2.65 miles (2 2/3rds miles or 4.26 km) from George IV.

Following an outbreak of elm disease at the beginning of WWII, in 1943, the avenue at the northern end was felled and work began on 30th August of that year, with the entire replanting completed by February 1946.

The northern end of the avenue as we know it today, dates from that time, and is planted with London Plane and Horse Chestnuts. The original plan was to decide after a period of thirty years or so which species to retain, but during the subsequent thinning in the 1970s, the mix was replaced.

The Long Walk in the early 1900's. Many of the trees by this time were in need of replacement.

The Long Walk near Windsor Castle before the old trees were
cut down in 1943 and replaced with young saplings.

The view north towards the Castle in 2000.

Gerald at Windsor Castle with a tourist standing by me 1965.

'On Sentry at Windsor Castle 1965', next to Gerald a young tourist, standing to attention.

(Author of photo unknown).

The Bank of England Picket, January morning 1958.

I can remember many Guard Duties at the Bank of England. The Guards for the Bank had to march from Wellington Barracks through the rush hour all the way to the Bank, which took some time. This was done in all weather as shown in this photo, and was completed after the Guard Mount and Inspection.
When we arrived at the Bank we could relax for a while, while the Old Guard handed over its responsibility to the New Guard. The Sentry Post Roster for the night was then given, two hours on and four off, throughout the night.

The Accommodation was quite comfortable; we had a television, nice kitchen and comfortable beds.
Whilst on Sentry Duty, you were required to patrol the corridors of the Bank and one of the most interesting things I found there were the pictures on the walls. These were of all the underground vaults with Gold Bullion stacked around six to eight feet high for as far as the eye can see! These corridors were lower than the London Underground Railway, and I did hear, if the Bank was ever broken into, these corridors could be flooded, but that could just be hearsay and may not in fact be true.
The Security was so tight. There were keys for keys and Security Guards everywhere, including ourselves. Of course, in those days they did not have such sophisticated cameras as we have today.

The Guards had a special payment for working at the Bank and received Seven Shillings and Sixpence (37 and a half pence in today's money) and these were uncirculated coins straight from the Royal Mint.
The following morning we would prepare for the New Guard. Everything had to be spotless on handover and had to thoroughly clean the Guard Room and Kitchen, as though they were dirty.
We then prepared ourselves for the long march back to Wellington Barracks.

Chapter (7).
It was Ceremonial Duties at Windsor, when I met and Married June.

In the spring of 1964 I went on leave, and because I wanted to show my mother, took all my Ceremonial Guards Uniform with me. I secretly went to my bedroom and dressed in my uniform, and when I came down and surprised her she thought it wonderful to see me. She was thrilled at what I done, her son in a Guards Tunic, especially as before she met Dad she'd gone out with a Coldstream Guards Officer. Mum went on to inform me a close friend of hers, Mrs. Wherritt, who lived in the village had married a Grenadier, who had either died rather young or been killed, and said she would like to see me in my uniform, so I marched around to her house and knocked on the door. Her son answered the door and explained he could not let me in as they had important guests for dinner. Mrs. Wherritt came to the door and cried when she saw me dressed as I was, and was delighted that I had taken the time to go around and show her.

There were photographs taken that day but I'm afraid I no longer appear to have them. I'm still in touch with the Wherritt family, who have promised to see if they still have them.

Anyway, to go on with my story. As you will find out later it doesn't stop there, as the important guests I did not see, Margaret and Norman Broady, turned out to be a couple that twenty years later, became our neighbours!

Some years later, having got to know them rather well, I was telling them about this event and they remarked, 'Oh my God! We were the guests that day and watched you through the windows!'

Later that same year, I can remember being on Street Lining during Trooping the Colour and became aware of someone touching my back. I could also feel movement around my waist, and then a beautiful girl suddenly came around to my front, gave me a wink and said, 'phone me!'

When I returned to barracks, I found she'd written her telephone number in thick red lipstick on my white Buff belt! I did ring her, but not for what she had in mind, but to tell her what a Pratt I thought she was for ruining my belt as I had to clean all my kit including my belt and was not at all happy with what she had done.

I got my own back on girls though, and one day, whilst on duty at St James's Palace, chatted up seven of them out of the corner of my mouth and made dates with them all on the same corner near the Wellington Barracks gates. At the time in question we would be coming off duty and going past this corner on the coach to return to barracks, and the whole Guard waved at them from the coach as we went past.

The following year 1965, as I loved dancing, I went to the Carlton Dance Hall in Slough and met June Montrose Parker. At the time I was standing on the balcony with a pint in my hand looking down onto the dance floor. Here I saw a gorgeous girl dancing and thought, 'I'm going to take her home tonight!' I later went down to the floor and asked her to dance, and ended up Jiving all night! There then followed a nice smooch at the last dance, which clinched it for me and asked to take her home, and a couple of kisses in her porch left me smitten, I was in heaven! I asked to see her the following day and we started going out together. She later invited me to her parent's home, as at that time she was living in digs, and on the way became rather worried and hope they would like me.

This is my Lovely June at 25.

A photo of June aged 25 when I met her at the dance. This was
taken in a booth on our way home from the first night we met in June 1965.

At the beginning of 1966 the Battalion was flying out to be posted in Germany.
June was born on 15th of June, hence her name, while I was born the same year in November, and we have this little joke that as she is six months older than me, I'm her 'Toy-Boy.'
Because I was to be posted away from Britain for so long, I was anxious not to lose her, so before I went, I asked her to marry me.
She said, 'Yes!' I was over the moon! We married just before Christmas on the 18th December 1965, and I flew out to Germany soon after.
As I wanted to show my new wife where I was born and where I spent my childhood, we spent a short weekend on honeymoon in Bristol at a 'B & B.'
Here we found some remarkable coincidences, June's middle name is Montrose, and we stayed at the Montrose Hotel, and as we were laying in bed one night having just turned off the lights, June remarked her father had said, 'Roses all the way!' This was because there were roses on the wedding cake and roses on the wall of their home. I quickly reached for the light switch, only to find we'd both reached for it together because we'd realised there were flowers on the walls of this hotel as well. As we both switched on our lights, we found roses on these walls as well. So, it's 'Roses all the way!'
As the 'B & B' was in Clifton, it was only natural to take June to see the Bristol Suspension Bridge spanning the Avon Gorge, then went on to the Victoria Rooms and Water Fountains.

The Bristol Clifton Suspension Bridge and the Gorge;   (Photo by Richard Olpin)

Gerald with the bridge behind him.

Gerald & June on honeymoon at the Clifton Suspension Bridge Bristol, 1965.

Bristol Suspension Bridge & we called on David my brother at Filton. 19th December 1966.

The Victoria Rooms, Waterfall at Clifton. June looked so happy, I can't believe we were Married.

Chapter (8)

When I flew out to Germany in 1966, I was looking forward to June joining me as soon as she could, but it wasn't until March that same year before I was allocated a Married Quarter. But, there was a hitch, as I would be away on manoeuvres on the day she was due to arrived. This meant I had to take over the accommodation early, and had everything ready for when she arrived. To make her feel more at home, I'd bought her a few gifts, a large pink Teddy Bear and some nice L.P's, one of which was a Frank Ifield double album, which in later years he actually signed, and will explain about that later in the book.
I was a little upset as I would not be there to see her face when she found these gifts.
Anyway, when I eventually arrived home at the flat some days later, she wasn't there! I went everywhere looking for her, but had no luck in finding her!
It turned out she'd met my best mate, George Green's wife on the flight out, who was also on her way to be with her husband, and he was on the same manoeuvres as me!
They got on really well and rather than both being on there own, June moved into her flat for a week until I got home. That was great as it meant I was able to carry her over the threshold as well as get to see her face when opened her presents. Oh! and I got a Baby doll nightdress, I could not wait to see her in that.

June and Gerald in Wuppertal Town Square September 1966.
We know this as June was three months pregnant when this picture was taken.

Just prior to June flying out to Germany I took my Driving Test in a Land Rover, and the Testing Officer, Captain Dobson, took me into Wuppertal for this exam. As I drove around the city I followed his instructions, turn left here, turn right there and seemed to be driving for ages until he at last told me to return to Barracks.

I had been to Wuppertal on many occasions with my own Driving Instructor, and while we were there had passed through a part of the city that was being changed from a one way system into a two way system as a temporary measure during modernisation, and went that way. As we proceeded, Captain Dobson noticed some of the old signs still in place and shouted, 'Stop! You're going down a one way street!' 'No Sir' I replied. 'We are not! This is a two way system,' and pointed out the signs written in German stating this fact. When he realised his mistake he apologised, then said, 'I think I had better give you a pass!'
'Yahoo! A Pass!'

A couple of weeks later we were off on exercise again, this time to Padderborne. As I had recently passed my driving test, I was now going on a course to become a Ferret Scout Car driver. At the time, I was an Officer's Batman, who would soon become our Platoon Commander, and me his driver. After the course we were off to Sennelager for manoeuvres, and were expected to be away for around a month. Because of this, some of our Married Personal was allowed to return to Harding Barracks, Wuppertal each weekend in the back of a three ton truck, this we named: 'The Passion Wagon!'

I was over the moon! A few weeks after the end of the exercise June told me she was pregnant! And our son Graham was born on the 17th February the following year. I was so proud of our beautiful baby, my beautiful 'Passion Wagon Sennelager Baby!'

One evening, when June was around eight months pregnant, I arrived home from barracks and found her scrubbing the house from top to bottom, and became rather cross as she shouldn't be doing something like that in her condition. Later that evening she complained of bad pains in her back and being naive told her not to worry, she had most likely strained her back doing the cleaning.

Well, at two o'clock in the morning she was still in pain, and getting them every ten to fifteen minutes, so I rang the doctor, who immediately sent an Ambulance to take us to Esselohn Military hospital about thirty miles away.

The driver was only a young chap and sat with him in the cab while June lay in the back. We had to drive some thirty miles to the hospital, and around half way there climbed in the back as June was having these pains more often, which were now happening every two or three minutes! That's when I realised she was having the baby!

We arrived at the hospital between three in the morning, and thankfully everyone was waiting for us.

The nurse said, 'everything's fine' and sent me home saying she would not have the baby yet. I would have like to see it being born. 'It' being the optimal word not knowing if it were a boy or girl, as in those days it wasn't the norm, plus I think the nurse didn't want me there either.

I finally arrived home between 5 o'clock in the morning and rang the hospital. They said she was in labour, and to call back later. I then rang back at 6 o'clock to be told, 'It's a boy!' who weighed in at six pounds ten ounces, and was born at 5-45am I was ecstatic! And when I went into Barracks at 8 O'clock I was running around calling to everyone, 'It's a boy, it's a boy!' and within an hour, the entire barracks knew L/Cpl Griffiths had a Son!

Hi'ya here at last.

Hope she knows what she's doing.

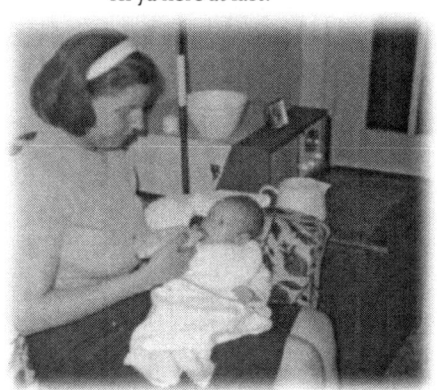

Ah, that's better.

This wind is killing me.

Our Graham beginning to get about.

Graham's first Christmas, and as they were away from their homes and their families in Germany on Christmas day I invited three of my mates to come for Christmas Dinner.

From left to right: Terry Ingram, L/Cpl Gaz Gallagher who went on to become a Warrant Officer holding Graham, then Guardsman Alan Urvoy, who went on to be a L/Sgt Non Commissioned Officer. It is great as to this day Gaz, Alan and myself are still in contact with each other and they are all great Guys who I don't see enough of. Gaz, finished his Army Career and he became a Prison Officer, while Alan finished his Career and became a Police Officer, but sadly lost touch with Terry Ingram.

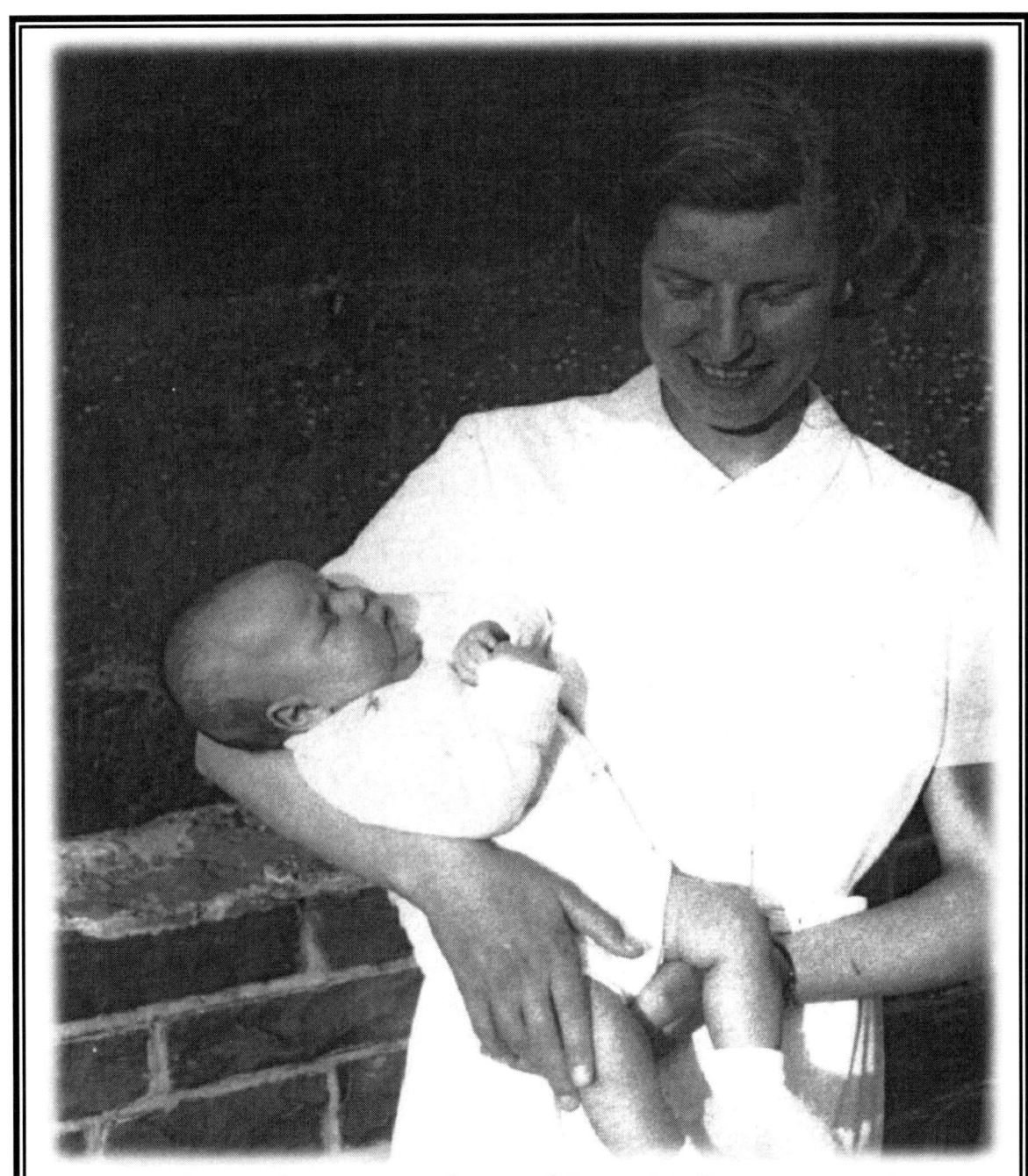

Graham three months and June in Germany 1967.

We named him Graham John Griffiths after my eldest brother, 'Graham Emanuel Griffiths', Graham Senior, and for a middle name chose John after June's Dad, 'John Leslie Parker'.
'Oh! And Graham was June's Mother's Maiden name.

MINI REVIVAL

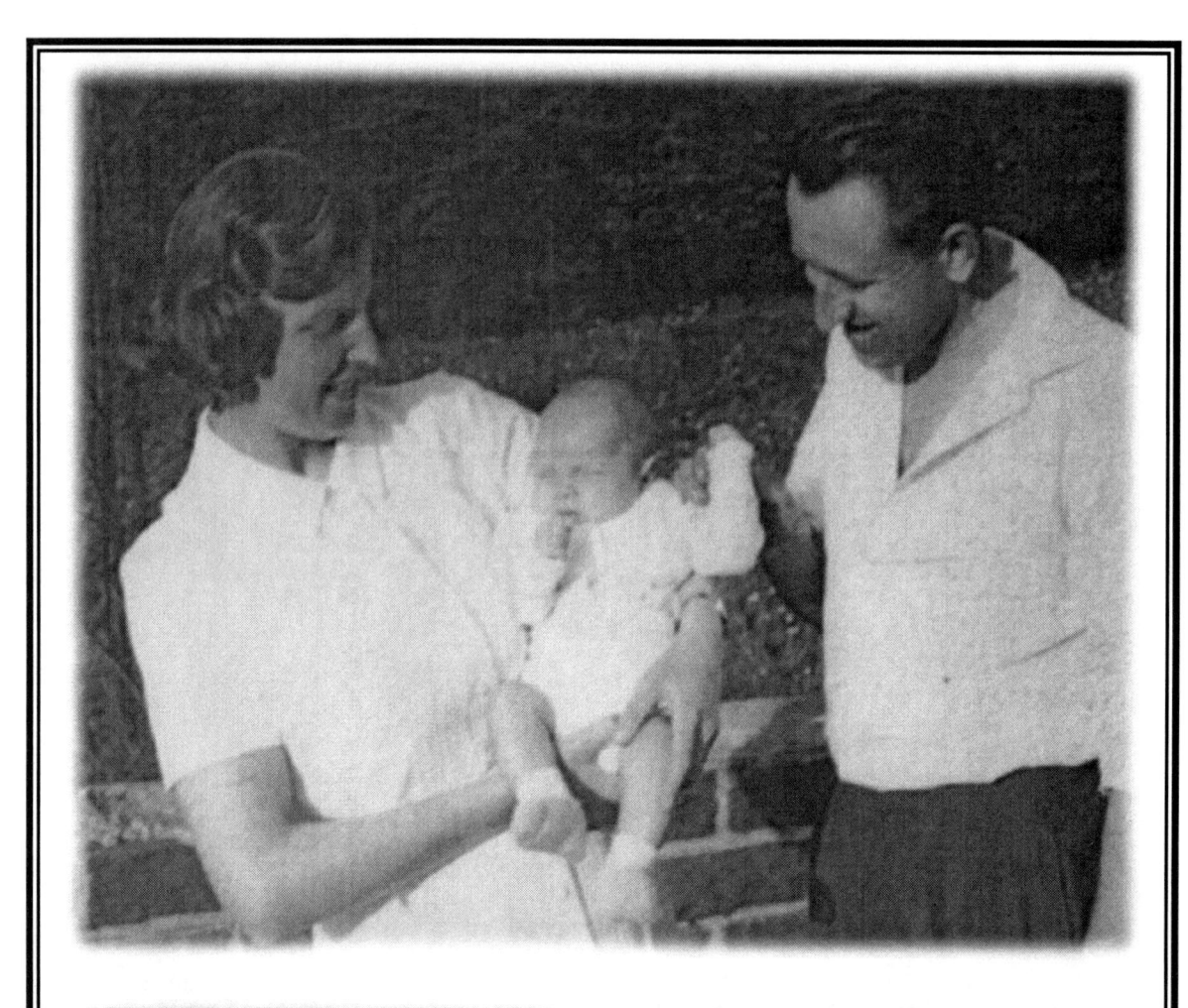

A MAN who bought a Mini car 18 years ago in West Germany, but sold it soon after has bought it again — after spotting it in Tesco's car park in Quedgeley!

Gerald Griffiths bought the car for £414 in 1968 from the manufacturer's factory in Cologne, West Germany, when he was stationed there in the Grenadier Guards.

Gerald (44), of The Rea Bridge House, Elmore Lane, Quedgeley, sold it two years later to a couple in Stroud after bringing it over from West Germany.

Gerald, the bridge keeper at Rea Bridge, thought that was the last he would ever had ever bought.

But to his amazement he spotted it last year in Tesco's car park in Quedgeley — and later bought it from Mrs. Pauline Lambert, of Berkeley Close, Cashes Green, Stroud, for £175.

Gerald plans to use it to teach his son, Graham (19), an assistant at McDonalds in Gloucester, how to drive.

The car is still in good working order and Gerald plans to work on it to keep it in tip-top condition.

Said Gerald: "It was the first brand new car that I ever bought. When I saw it again in the car park at Quedgeley I recognised it

Back in the driving seat... Graham Griffiths, now 19, and (inset) at the wheel of th

Correction in the paper it was bought in 1967 sold it in 1970 which was three years later.

I had to go forwards 18 years in time just to show this picture.

Graham's first car and he actually learned to drive in it when he was old enough.

Graham is now 43 and sadly the Morris Mini has gone to that
Great scrapyard in the sky.

This picture was taken when we came home from Germany to show Graham off to our Family. They were in Slimbridge at that time.

When we came home from Germany, I was driving the Morris Mini you have just seen, and drove it all the way home. We also brought a German friend with us, and dropped her off at a Army Camp on Saulsbury-Plain, at two oclock in the morning, then went on to Gloucester.

After we had dropped her off, I called at a garage for petrol, then drove along a road with rather sharp bends for around two or three miles. After coming out of these bends ,we followed a long straight section and could see lights coming towards us and thought, 'these lights are on the wrong side of the road!' Then realised it was me driving on the right instead of the left! I quickly pulled over to the correct side of the road just as a large Juggernaut went flying past and thought. 'Goodness me! How long have I been driving on the wrong side of the road?' I then realise it was after getting petrol and leaving the garage around four or five miles back and before going around those bends.

I felt so bad I had to stop, and was violently sick at the thought of what could have happened had we met the truck on the bends. It would have gone right over us and kept going! God must certainly have been watching over us that night as my wife, baby son Graham and myself would have been no more, and our two lovely Grandchildren, Larrisa and Brandon, would never have been born. It really doesn't bear thinking about, and of course, I would not be writing about it today.

Gerald holding Graham up to show him off, at Slimbridge when we came home.

Graham getting bigger.

At the Funfair near Wuppertal, Germany.

At the Funfair near Wuppertal, Germany.

Photo taken at Graham's first Christmas Party at Harding Barracks, Wuppertal.

Now walking very well, and ready to go out on the town, in Munster, Germany.

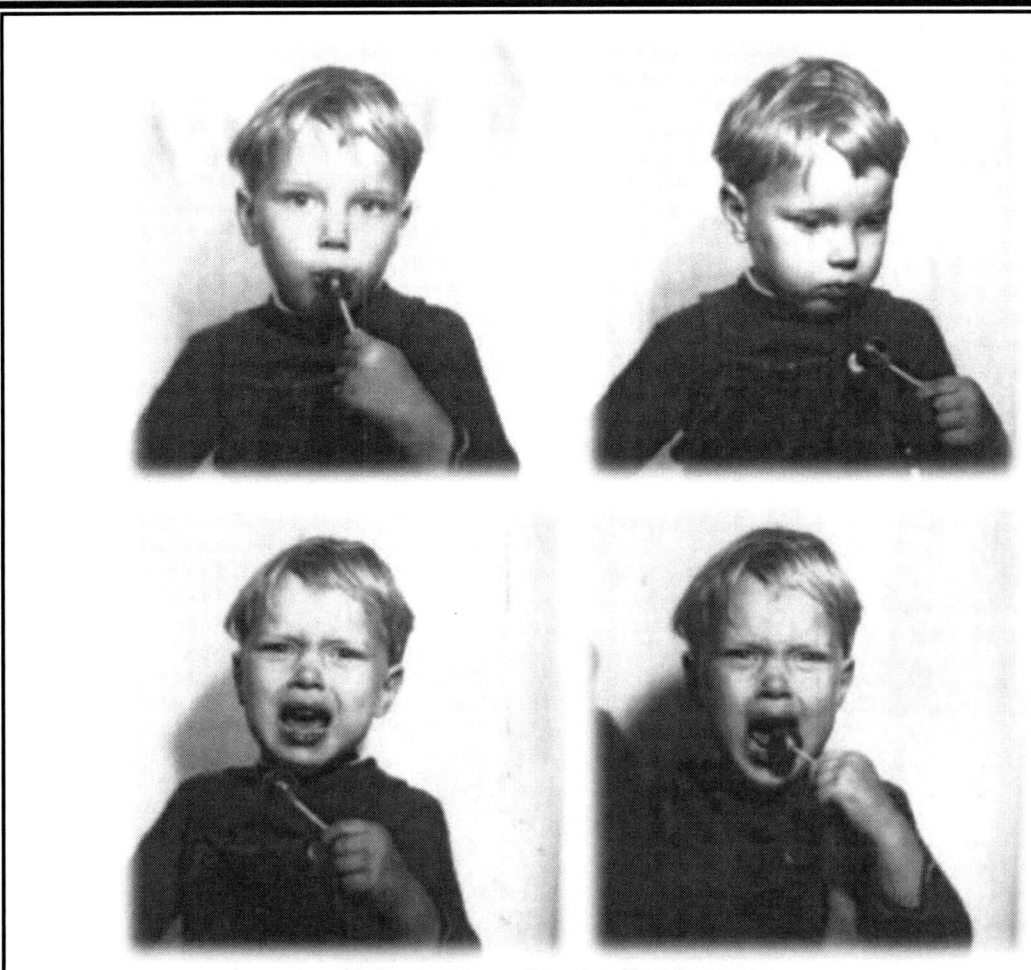

Graham did not like the flashing camera.

Graham loved this little car.

Graham aged one year ½. Spotty Dog went everywhere.
We still have it to this very day.

I just love this picture he's such a happy boy.

June and I love him dearly.

June outside our local Pub eating house, called, 'The Wickuler Biere', this is where we all used to hang out, it was just over the road where we lived, and just down the road from the barracks.

Back at Harding Barracks and what's going on. First are Sgt Majors and Drill Sgt's.

D/Sgt Jack Thomas.   Sgt Major Ray Huggins M.B.E.   A/D/Sgt Robert Woodfield.

This is the 2nd Battalion Grenadier Guards, Corps of Drums at Wuppertal.

Photos thanks to Mrs Jill Shelly

2nd Grenadier Guards Corps of Drums. Practicing on the square at Harding Barracks, Wuppertal.

Photo by David Higgs.

**The 2nd Battalion Grenadier Guards Corps of Drums.
On Sports day 1967.**

Photo by David Higgs.

Gerald driving a Reconnaissance Ferret Scout Car.
Note! 30m 1919 4 Browning Machine-Gun above his head.

Chapter (9).   Gerald in Recognisance's Platoon.

This same year of 1966, after obtaining my position as a Ferret Scout Car driver, we also attended a shooting exercise and drove to Volgesang, which is situated close to the Sieg Fried Line on the borders of Western Germany and Belgium. The Mowschau and Volgesang have such beautiful countryside with breathtaking mountain ranges and valleys, and is a very wintery part of Germany, with a wild corner of very icy river lakes and woodlands.

Photo by David Higgs

A photograph of the firing ranges on the lakes at Vogelsang. Whilst there, we practiced firing the 30m 1919 mk 4 Browning Machine Gun from our Ferret Scout Cars as well as firing our personal weapons, the S.L.R's and G.P.M.G's.
In the centre foreground, with hand on hip, can be seen Guardsman David Higgs, talking to L/Cpl Fee. I am standing to the left next to the soldier leaning over the rail and looking over my right shoulder. Two Ferret Scout Cars, plus a Saracen Armoured Personal Carrier can be seen at the lakeside, from which we took turns firing the Browning Machine Guns from their Turrets.

**A smoke break and stopping for dinner. The only other person I recognise in this picture is
L/Sgt Kit Green, on the left just behind me. The soldier behind him is most likely
Sgt Vassa Campbell, while the soldier with his back to camera is believe to be David Higgs.**

As a matter of interest. Around the woodlands, lakes and townships of Volgasang there is quaint little villages with timber framed house as well as Chateaus and Castles that can be seen nestling in this beautiful mountain range.

But, on the darker side, Volgasang was a place where Hitler set up his elite training camps, and the one we stayed in during our visit, was used as a Stud Farm during the 2nd World War to perpetuate his Arian Race. In those days it beggars belief what these beautiful places were used for, while today, many of these camps, Castle and Chateaus have now been turned into Museums.

Gerald & George Green. One of my mates in 1966.
George became a L/Sgt and later went on to become a Drill Sergeant.

During my service, Wuppertal in Germany is probably the place I was happiest, which was due to the fact that I now had a beautiful baby boy, which had given me a much more meaningful purpose to life, with more responsibilities. This resulted in me wanting the best for my wife June and son Graham. The life I had as a Batman to Captain Gray'Cheape, the Platoon Commander, I loved driving, and it is great fun driving the Ferret Scout Car. So nothing could compare to being in the recognisance section, out on the road and being your own boss.

During my service, I had a wide range of diverse responsibilities. These included: becoming a marksman with the Self Loading Rifle, (S.L.R.) as well as the, L.M.G. Light Machine Gun, (Bren gun) and General Purpose Machine Gun. (G.P.M.G.)

Whilst serving with the Anti Tank Platoon, I also fired their 'Wombat' and 'Mobat' Anti Tank weapons. While in the Reconnaissance, I also drove 'Captain Gray'Cheape, our Commander's, Ferret Scout Car and was also his Batman, Radio Operator and Browning Machine Gunner. I also served in England, Guyana and Germany.

These two Photo's by David Higgs.

David Higgs, Sgt Vassa Campbell, and Edd a Mechanic, and Sgt Campbell in the Turret.

It was great fun driving the Ferret scout car. Although small, it was very fast and had four gears both backwards and forwards, and would go just as fast in each direction. It also had a double declutch, which was similar to the clutch's on ordinary bus's at that time.

These were pre-selecting gears. To engage these, you would select first gear and stamp the clutch down, then select second, ready for when you reached the correct speed. When this was achieved, you simply stamped on the clutch and selected third and so on until you reached fourth.

On reaching and driving in fourth gear you would select first ready in the event of an emergency stop, especially if the enemy were to your front. When this happened, you would quickly stamp your foot and select reverse all at the same time, then race backwards all in one movement. You could go through the same procedure when going backwards and we used to have races to see who could do it the fastest over a given point. This could be great fun and prepared us in becoming efficient drivers.

Sennelager. Sgt Alan Blackburn starting a cooking stove, Gerald just back from the loo, ha-ha. And having a well earned rest.

Photo by David Higgs.

In the front, our Reconnaissance Platoon Commander, Captain Gray'Cheape.
Next Sgt Alan Blackburn, our Mechanic. Behind him from the left,
Gerald Griffiths, George Green, David Higgs, Behind them, Mick Fee, Alan Urvoy, Alf Sharman.

Ferret Fox Scout Car.
The Turret is fitted with a 30 m 1919 4 Browning Machine-Gun.
There are six grenade launchers on the wings of the hull
Also a 7.62 MM. G.P.M.G. could be mounted

This picture of George Green standing in front of his Ferret Scout car is not so clear that is why I kept it small, and I can remember this picture being taken as though it was yesterday, I remember we'd hidden our Ferret Scout Cars in a barn right by these very building.

**Reconnaissance's Group. Top three: Sergeant's Steve Marshal, Jim Scott and L/Cpl Mike Fee.
Middle row: George Green, Alan Urvoy, Alf Sharman, Sergeant Kit Green.
Front row: Sergeant Alan Hughes, Alan Blackburn, Gerald Griffiths, L/Sgt Vassa Campbell.**

One of the most outstanding athletes of whom I admired, in the 2nd Battalion was Sgt Alan Hughes. He is in the Photo on the left, his ability on the discus and hammer was amazing. I did hear 'by hearsay', that he threw the discus on the square at Wuppertal in 1966, during practice and cleared the Olympic record, but it was not recorded, as there were not enough witnesses.

He was also a very good swimmer, but I can remember beating him in the back stroke once, when in Guyana. He also became a Sgt Commander in Recognisance Platoon.

We also had a very good boxing team, as Sgt Major Huggins was a very keen fan of boxing, so those boxing had all the time they wanted to train in the gym, and would be cleared of duties while training.

I remember a very outstanding Boxer that was in the team whose name was George Lloyd. He was in our Platoon when we passed through Basic Training at the Depot at Pirbright, all his wins were knockout.

Photo by David Higgs.
Some of the lads on a FV 432 Personal Carrier, and David Higgs's Camouflaged Ferret Scout Car.

Photo by Captain Cray 'Cheap.

Gerald having a well earned rest during the excersise, alongside his Ferret Scout Car. Do you remember chapter five page 107 in the book about the Rattle Snake that was under the camp bed in Guyana? Well this is the same type of camp bed, and shows how closs to the ground they are. If Dave had put his feet over the side he would have been bitten for sure.
I was so comfortable I could have stayed there all day. But no such luck! I had to go out not long after that on a Reconnasence Patrol with Captain Gray'Cheape.

Captain Gray'Cheape Platoon Commander.   Photo by Capt Gray 'Cheap.

Captian Gray'Cheape our Platoon Commander on our Ferrit Scout Car. Not long after we had to go out on a reconnicence patrol. During this patrol, I remember that Captain Gray'Cheape had to go on a recce with maps etc and I was driving him over reasonably rough ground. At the time we were driving up a rather steep slope at the side of a hill and could feel the top side of the wheels lifting of the ground, plus the steering going light. Knowing the Ferret Scout Car is top heavy, I felt sure it was going to tip over.

I somehow managed to stop the vehicle against the side of a tree! My thoughts being, if it tips it will lean against the tree. Captain Gray'Cheape shouted 'what have you stopped for?' To which I replied, 'I thought we were going to tip over Sir.' He then came back and answered, 'Oh, when in doubt, more power on the accelerator, keep going, we have to get back!'

I then started to slowly move off and as we were still climbing I think, Captain Gray'Cheape realised how close we were to tipping over, so he decided to have me drive into the hill off the pathway, and go back down.

As he had to attend a debriefing we had to return to camp reasonably quickly. Again we found ourselves on extremely rough ground with large water filled ruts, which I had to negotiate and ease my vehicle over, I was only thinking of the comfort of my Commander as he was standing in the Turret, and I was sitting down. However, Captain Gray'Cheape bellowed, 'don't worry about me', get back and get a move on!' I really felt for him because I could hear him yell, and knew he'd been banged about against the metal turret of the Ferret Scout Car; we did however arrive back in plenty of time.

I have the utmost respect for Captain Gray'Cheape, and I know for sure speaking for the rest of the Recce Platoon he was a damned good Platoon Commander. I was only speaking the other day with David Higgs, he was actually saying the same thing, and what a great time we had in recognisance.

This is a photo of the really rough barren landscape at Sennelager which was a part of the training area,
I was driving Captain Gray 'Cheap over to get back to camp in the Ferret Scout Car.

Photo by David Higgs.

Left to Right: L/Cpl Jim Scott, behind him Gerald Griffiths, Sgt Steve Marshal, Alan Urvoy.
Three in the rear, with the cigarette Vassa Campbell, then, Alf Sharman and David Higgs.

This photograph shows the lads on a large NATO exercise. At the time we were moving into a dense wood during the night. At the same time, Armoured Scout Cars, F.V.603 Saracens, and FV 432 tracked Armoured Personal Carriers, were also being directed into the woods by torches as none of these vehicle were allowed to show lights!

However, a luckless Saracen driver, who had arrived earlier, camouflaged his vehicle and deciding to have a rest, leaned against a tree and promptly fell asleep. In the meantime, a tracked 432 Personal Carrier was being directed towards where he lay, and in the dark, those responsible were unable to see him.

Luckily for him it had been raining all day as this vehicle reversed it ran him over, squashing his legs into the sodden wet ground, resulting in what was seen as only minor damage.

Had it not been raining that day his legs would have been mangled beyond recognition? He was eventually air lifted to hospital by helicopter and found to have suffered a fractured pelvis.

You can see how lucky he was by the next few photographs of FV 432's.

F.V. 432 Armoured Personal Carrier.    **F.V. 603 Saracen six wheeled Carrier.**

Photo by Richard Thomas Godfrey.
Sgt Richard Thomas Godfrey outside his Camourflaged FV432 Armour Personal Carrier.

Not so lucky for a man who had died on the autobahn on our way to a NATO exercise. At the time the entire Battalion was travelling in convoy as we drove towards Frankfurt. I was driving my Ferret Scout Car with the Commander in the turret and there were approximately forty or fifty vehicles all travelling in the same direction. Obviously, there would have been long gaps between the vehicles, and these would be in groups of four, five or six vehicles some twenty to twenty five yards apart.

Although I was unable to see what actually happened, I thought I saw something flying in the air and come back down about three vehicles ahead of me, then suddenly noticed one of the Saracen Armoured Personal Carriers veer off the autobahn, crash over the side and disappear.

It is said the Sergeant Commander L/Sgt Hadfield had tried to jump clear, but the vehicle rolled down on top of him and ended up crushed from the waist down. This incident stunned us all and he later died in the arms of one of his best mates, Sgt Tom Martin, a Police Sergeant at the time. The driver of the carrier was also badly hurt. He received a fractured skull, apparently the drivers hatch had came down on the drivers head. Not only did the Commander die in that accident, but the driver received a fractured skull and later, in hospital, had a metal plate fitted. During this accident I was instructed to park on the side of the autobahn, and was told to stay with my vehicle. It would appear that too many people at the site would be a hindrance.

This entire episode was such a tragedy, not only in him dying, but his dear wife was almost nine months pregnant as well and would now, never get to know his child.

L/Sgt Hadfield was well liked, and later buried with full military honours, where almost the entire Battalion turned out to pay their last respects, complete with a twenty one gun salute. He had not served with our Regiment that long, and had transferred from another regiment only a short while previously from the Guards Depot.

The F.V. 603 Saracen. This is a six wheeled vehicle, and the crew would typically be a driver and Commander, plus a troop commander and eight fully armed soldiers. Most carriers would have a turret mounted 30 mm Browning Machine Gun or 303 Bren Gun. These vehicles would also be fitted with two way radios. The F.V. 432 was very much the same, with the exception of it being a track vehicle.

Whilst on this same exercise, I was travelling down the road behind a Tank when it decided to stop. As I could not go around, or see past it to see why it had stopped, but knew it had stopped near a bridge. The next moment the turret opened, and the Commander began shouting and waving to a man leaning on a gate to a field. I was unable to understand what was said as they were shouting in German, but did hear the German shout back 'Swine hunt!' The commander then disappeared inside his tank and closed the turret.

Seconds later, the Tank began to roar into life, and as it went forward it started to lurch back and forth for a moment. It soon became apparent why, as there to my front was a mangled flattened car, which I just managed to get around. Apparently, the Commander had asked him to move it, but the farmer had told him to 'F' off in German, and refused to comply with his request.
As this was an extremely realistic exercise, the Commander could not be bothered with his insults and promptly carried on. I would like to point out the Tank was not a Grenadier's vehicle.
I'm unaware if my Commander Captain Gray 'Cheape remembers this incident? I will have to ask him.

5 Platoon 2 Company in the north of Germany 1966-67.

These exercises are usually extremely realistic. There are helicopters, jets and a host of other different forces involved. I remember I was one of three Ferret Scout Cars, crossing a field and suddenly heard an almighty 'Bang!' The next I saw was a Jet disappearing into the distance and the Ariel of my Ferret Scout Car swinging back and forth in its slipstream. My heart thumped and appeared to be jumping out of my chest. It had buzzed us, and was now officially classed as dead!

There were also bombers involved. These dropped bags of flour, as though they were bombs, the effects as they hit the ground were truly amazing. Due to being buzzed, the umpires put us out of the race, and for some time after could not be involved with the exercise.

I remember Captain Gray 'Cheap managed to cadge a ride in one of these Jets and thoroughly enjoyed it.

Myself and one of my best mate's on the Left Alan Urvoy in Germany 1966.

Picture of one of the Paderborn barracks blocks in the winter.

Gerald Moving a three tonner down by the L.A.D. in Harding Barracks Wuppertal.

Captain Gray 'Cheap once organised a trip to Amsterdam, and a tour to the brewery of Amstel's Beer. It was great and we all got to taste all the different Lager's, needless to say, we were half cut and two sheets to the wind, it was a fabulous day, and I will remember these good times for the rest of my life.

In the picture, on the adge of the Amsterdam Canal, left to right: Captain Gray 'Cheape, Guardsmen Alf Sharman, L/Cpl Mike Fee, L/Sgt Alan Maslin, L/Sgt Vassa Campbell, Guardsmen's Alan Urvoy, Gerald Griffiths, Mel Parker, and David Higgs. The ranks are as they were that day. Amstel's Brewery was founded 11 June 1870, and was named after the Amstel River. The brewery is now a University College. Amstel's Beer is still going strong, but under the brand name of Heineken Beer.

Gerald becoming a Non-Commissioned Officer.

After my son Graham was born, as she suffers with epilepsy, June went through a bad time with her health. It was then I decided to look for a job that would keep me around the Barracks rather than going away all the time and applied for the position of Battalion Pioneer.
This mainly consisted of keeping on top of repairs needed in and around the barracks. I had always been good with my hands, as well as good at my job and managed to get this position. Shortly after that the Pioneer Sergeant, one 'Cloggy' Homes, suggested I attend a Non Commissioned Officers Course.
It felt such a shame, I so enjoyed being in Reconnaissance, missed my mate's and working with Captain Gray 'Cheap as well as going on manoeuvres they attended.

In 1967, whilst stationed at Wuppertal, I became a Non Commissioned Officer, and being in the Armed Forces and now a Non Commissioned Officer, meant so much to me. On looking back at my time in the Grenadier Guards I find it full of fond memories. You tend to forget the bad times, and just remember the good ones, and I find, discipline, flexibility, punctuality, and organisation skills now come easy to me. All those years of dedication, fitness, practice of Martial Arts, and confidence in the gym. With this in mind, I want to pass on all my knowledge, within the writings of this book.

So, within a short time, I had completed my Non Commissioned Officer's Course, and passed with flying colours, and to the newly appointed L/Cpl Griffiths, things were now looking good.

As previously stated, I was now working in the Pioneers Shop in Wuppertal's Harding Barracks, mainly as a carpenter.
One particular day, one of our Drill Sergeants came into the shop and asked if I could repair his pace-stick, I replied that I could, and was pleased with the result as I'd made a rather good job of it. I thought 'Hey! I could make some of these to sell', which I did. These were made from old pickaxe handles by sawing the shaft lengthways. I also managed to obtain some small scraps of brass, and cut them to make the measuring part when extending the stick for marching. I believe I made around three of them.

While at Wuppertal I had some Guard Duties in the Guard Room at Harding barracks,
and as L/Cpl, N.C.O. of the Guard

During this time at Harding Barracks, I remember one particular incident that happened not long after we first arrived and involved four or five Officers who had ordered and bought Mercedes sports cars, which had been delivered, that week. Captain Gray'Cheape had ordered one himself, but is not the Officer I am about to tell you about.
As they celebrated the delivery of these vehicles in the Officer's Mess, one of these Officers, who had far too much to drink, decided to take his for a drive.
The Commanding Officer refused to allow him to do this, and ordered him not to go. To which the Officer replied, 'I am going anyway!' and while this young Officer went to his car to drive to the main gates, the Commanding Officer rang the Guard Room and told them to lock the gates and not allow him out of barracks.
When the Officer arrived, the Sergeant of the Guard was waiting. He then ordered the Sergeant to open the gates. 'Sorry Sir' he replied, 'I can't do that as the Commanding Officer has ordered me to shut them and not let anyone out!' The officer then informed him he was ordering him to do so. To which the Sergeant replied, 'Sorry sir, but the Commanding Officers orders overrides yours', and promptly refused to comply with his order.
The young Officer, in temper, frustration and having had too much to drink, turned his car around and drove down to the other end of the barracks. Here he turned at the roundabout and accelerated back towards the main gates. It was estimate his speed was in excess of one hundred miles an hour when he hit the gates taking them off their hinges and carrying then up the road some few yards. These gates were some ten feet high and approximately seven yards across, and constructed of four inch box steel.
I'm not sure how badly he was hurt, but, do recall he was posted back to England soon after. I also remember a mechanic, who I know quite well and was one of our L.A.D. detachments (Light Aid Detachment) who bought the wrecked sports car. He also had a very old classic Mercedes like the one's the German high ranking officers used in the S.S. during the 2nd World War, the ones with the running boards along the sides.
It was a beautiful black saloon and being a mechanic kept it in immaculate condition. He ended up taking the engine from this brand new wrecked car and putting it in this car, such a modern engine in such a very old car, amazing!

Not long after the battalion moved to Munster in Germany I was still in the pioneer's shop hoping to be around the barracks more, but 'no', we were off on Manoeuvres again! Also attached to the Assault Pioneers, were members of the Corps of Drums. Here are a couple of photos of some of the lads and their FV 432's and FV 603 Saracens

This photo submitted by Richard Lee Nettleton.

Left to right: Richard Nettleton, David Smith, Dick Shelly, Barry Last and 'Spud' Sleight. Spud, who was our Battalion Pioneer Shop Equipment Repairer. I remember teaching him to drive when we got back to Chelsea Barracks London in 1969. We were driving to the rear of Chelsea barracks and someone was waiting to cross a zebra crossing, but Spud did not stop for them. There was no danger but the Police saw him commit this offence and pulled us over. They eventually let us go with a word of caution saying be careful next time.

Photo by Mrs Jill Shelly, wife of the Late 'Dick' Shelly, 'R.I.P.'

**Dick Shelly in the driving seat of his Fv 432, on the square at Munster.
We were just going or had just come back from our exercises, 1967-8.**

Photo thanks to, Mrs Jill Shelly.

'Dick' Charles Shelly driving, showing his driving skills as we are out in the front, I can't remember the other lads but I am in front on the right side of the vehicle. 1968. This actual photo appeared in a recruiting leaflet for the Grenadier Guards.

Photo thanks to Mrs Jill Shelly.

This is Gerald just got back from the exercise and about to get in his Mini that you can just see on the left of the this very old looking photo. This is the same Mini I was telling you about earlier. Dick Shelly, back at the barracks, on the square in Munster Germany, by his FV 432.

The 2nd Battalion Grenadier Guards on Parade at Munster Germany, 1968.

I was on this parade and remember the day very well. From the time I left the Recognisance and moved into the Pioneer Shop, instead of have anything to do with Ferret Scout cars, was now involved with F. V. 432 Armoured Personal Carrier's as part of the Assault Pioneer Section.

It was here at Munster on to this very square that Dick Shelly, one of the drivers and myself, who you've just seen in the last photos, were coming back from exercise onto this same square.

I remember the hard work involved in getting these vehicles lined up in straight lines, as can be seen in the photo. On the Square are: F. V. 603's Saracens six wheeled Carriers, F. V. 432's tracked Armoured Personal Carriers and Ferret Armoured Cars, known as Ferret Scout Cars. The Ferret being the vehicle I had so much experience with in Recognisance. It had a Rolls Royce B60 16 petrol engine of power/ weight 35. 1 hp/tonne and had 4 wheel drive. On a full tank it had a range of approximately 190 miles (310 Km) at a speed of 58 mph (93 km/h). There were also half track vehicles, which the M. T. used as there Maintenance vehicles.

This parade was part of the inspections of our vehicles by the Commanding Officer, for after a large exercise, all vehicles had to be thoroughly cleaned and remain spotless. After the inspection, the men performed a drive past in their vehicles with the Commanding Officer taking the Salute.

The F. V. 603 Saracen became a very recognised part of the Policing on the streets of Northern Ireland. The 2nd Battalion Grenadier's were on stand-by when those troubles started, so one minute they were training in Germany, then back to England for Ceremonial Duties and off to Ireland as a Peace Keeping Force.

Photos by kind permission Mrs Shelly.

Sadly Dick Shelly passed away in 1990.
Dick Shelly in Combat order, probably around 1968 at Munster when he was driving F. V. 432's Armoured Personal Carriers.
Then a young Richard 'Dick' Shelly in Drummers Tunic Order.

Below is Richard Lee Nettleton, the tallest Corps of Drums flute player on this Parade in full Ceremonial Dress.

Photo by kind permission, from Richard Nettleton.

These Photos go to show the extraordinary value of all Guardsmen in the Household Division's.

As you seen by the Parade photo, one minute you see Dick Shelly, Richard Nettleton, and the rest of the Battalion coming back from combat training in Armoured Personal Carriers, Ferret Scout Cars, etc:

Then into the Colourful Ceremonial role of guarding the British Royal Sovereignty and all that Britain stands for.

It being hard enough for Guardsmen to go from one discipline to the other, as in the discipline of marching and absolute meticulous correct positioning on changing the Guard at Buckingham Palace, but to be able to be part of the Corps of Drums, and having to practice your particular instruments, as well as the meticulous positioning of formation in the band.

This extraordinary work load go's to shows just how hard the Corps of Drums must work.

I hope in my writings I have been able to put across the elite excellence and the standards of the entire Household Division, which includes the Horse and Life Guards.

You can imagine their hard work as well, in having to groom their horses, plus polish the brass and straps of their bridle gear as well as their own uniforms.

Chapter (10).

In 1969 the Battalion returned to England , and back to London Duties, but just before they left my wife was taken ill and hospitalised, which meant I had to stay in Germany with the Rear Party.
I then returned a while later when she'd recovered, and drove my Mini all the way back to London and on into Chelsea Barracks. Then, after two weeks leave, it was back to Ceremonial Duties.
We were given a quarter to the rear of the Barracks at Stillington Street, but did not like it as it reminded us of a Prison Block, even the courtyard looked like a Prison, but we had to get on with our lives.
I did have a larger project while at Chelsea, I built flashing coloured ceiling lights over the bar in the Sergeants Mess, and made them out of egg-cartons and Christmas lights, and it looked quite good.

Photo kind permission by Gaz Gallagher.

This is a photo of the Pioneer's, my work mates. From left to right: Guardsman Wilkinson, Gdsm Richard Bird, L/Cpl Gaz Gallagher, L/Sgt Norman Askins, L/Cpl Gerald Griffiths, Gdsm Terry Ingram, and Gdsm Ray Jones.

Guardsman, Ray Jones was a brilliant artist, and would often draw cartoons which were so funny. I remember he did one of a man in a dentist chair, having his tooth pulled. If you can imagine a Dentist standing on the armrest, pulling hard on the tooth, his arms high in the air and a long strand of skin going from the tooth and pliers to this guys mouth. Picture this guy's stomach and groin all drawn in where his privates are and the roots of his tooth was so far down, it joined his testicles! His next picture was where there was a big pop, and you see the pliers go flying in the air with this long strand of skin flying all over the place with a pair of testicles on the end of it. But what were so funny were their facial expressions, and I would have given a week's wages to now own that picture. So if anyone out there knows of Ray's whereabouts, give me a call.

2nd Battalion Grenadier Guards changing Guard at Buckingham Palace. The St James's Palace Detachment, marching to St James's around 1969. I wonder if I was in that same guard.

On the left: The Master of Rollo. On the right: Captain Gray 'Cheape.

Photo with thanks to Captain, Gray 'Cheap.

Captain H.L. Gray 'Cheape.

The 'Brigade of Guards',

Regarding the contingent of Officer's in the Brigade. These are usually taken from the gentry of Britain where many families hold the tradition that their son, usually the eldest, will join the Guards and carry on the tradition of their forefathers. This is done with pride and dedication to the Regiment of their father.

An officer in the Guards has a strong possibility of becoming a high ranking dignitary within the dominion of the 'Household Division', and in making a man of him, which demanded respect, and someone to look up to, as a leader of men. I am a little biased as 'Captain Gray 'Cheape' was my Platoon Commander and one of the best Officers in the 2nd Battalion Grenadier Guards. He was a strong disciplinarian, as well as a fair discerning man of honour, who would fight in your corner if he thought you were in the right.
His family also held strong traditions as his father was also an ex Grenadier Guards Officer, and do believe he was a Colonel.
As you've read earlier in the book, I was his Batman and driver of his Fox Ferret Scout Car, and would have read some of the stories of us in the Reconnaissance Platoon.
There have been some great times during my service with him, and after I finished my service with the Guards in 1970, Captain Gray'Cheape went on to become the Regimental Adjutant.

Although I was always biddable to him, I never felt shackled or intimidated by him and when off duty, he was just a gentleman'.

As I said earlier in the book, the respect and discipline in the Guards is carried over into our Civilian lives, which appears to be lost in this day and age. There doesn't seem to be that respectful attitude as youngsters grow up today, that we, whether we were an Officer, Non Commissioned Officer or Guardsman once had.
These qualities were imparted into us through the discipline of the Guards Training.

Maybe if subscriptions should, or would be brought back, this could change things and could, and would be a good thing.

In my opinion, when National Service was abolished, this is where the decline in discipline in families started to breakdown. In our day, when a boy became a man, it would always coincide with him going in and coming out of the forces, he would go in at eighteen, 'as a boy' and come out as a man at twenty. In the army he would learn the respect for his elders, and pride in his appearance. I would not change any of my experiences of when I served in The Grenadier Guards for the world, as looking back on my life, these were exciting times, and was making something of myself.
Around 1965-66, the title Brigade of Guards was changed, and is now known as the 'Household Division'.

Captain Gray 'Cheape being presented to H.R.H the Queen.

During the April 1969 I was on Guard Duty at the Tower of London, and I had a Book of 'The Memoires of Sir Alexander of Tunis'. It was a gift from an ex-girlfriend of mine, which she sent to me in Guyana on my Birthday.

I had it on Guard with me and was showing it to the Captain of the Guard, who informed me the Governor of the Tower of London, was Lord Alexander, who was in residence at the time.
He said, 'If you go to his house on the Tower Green and do everything correctly when he answers the door, like standing to attention and saluting, and ask him nicely, I'm sure he would sign your book.'

I went to his house as directed, and he indeed answered the door, and when I explained why I was there he invited me in and wrote in my book: Kind Regards from Lord Alexander, to L/Cpl Griffiths all the very best in your career with the Grenadier Guards. This was just a few months before he died, but later that same year the book was stolen! I do know by whom, but as I could not prove it, will not mention the person's name.
Sometime after my service with the Guards had come to an end, I happened to be in London and called in to Chelsea Barracks, where a soldier I knew happened to be on Barrack Guard.

This was the same soldier I was talking about, who invited me back to his home, and while he was making tea, I glanced through his bookshelf and found the book on Lord Alexandra there on his shelf! I quickly flicked through the pages and found the page in his book, the one in my book that Lord Alexandra had signed was torn out, which was something of a coincidence. I never did say anything, come-c-come-sae, water under the bridge and all that. But I was very upset to have lost it, it was such a memorable gift, and one I could have cherished for many years.

Harold Alexander, 1st Earl Alexander of Tunis.

After the surrender of the Axis forces in Tunisia in May 1943, Alexander's Command became 15th Army Group, and under Eisenhower, was responsible for mounting the Allied Invasion of Sicily in July, once again controlling two armies:

Montgomery's Eighth Army and George S. Patton's U.S. Seventh Army. After Sicily 7th Army Headquarters was replaced by U.S. Fifth Army Headquarters under Mark Clark for the Allied invasion of Italy.

Lord Alexander of Tunis died of a perforated aorta on 16 June 1969. His funeral was held on 24 June 1969 at St Georges Chapel, Windsor Castle, and his remains are buried in the churchyard of Ridge, near Tyttenhanger, his family's Hertfordshire home. Lady Alexander died in 1977.

Also at the Tower of London, most people do not know about the ceremony of the Keys, which is performed each evening at ten o'clock at last Post.

The Tower Guard is paraded outside the guardroom when the Beefeater goes around locking all the Tower Castle doors & gate's for the night.

This ceremony has been carried out since the 14th century at exactly the same time at 9.53pm. The Chief Yeoman Warder, dressed in the Tudor Watch-coat, meets the Military Escort, which is made up of members of the Tower of London Guard. Together, the CYW and the Yeoman Warder 'Watchman', secure the main gates of the tower.

They then return to Water Lane by the Bloody Tower. The party is halted by the number one Sentry and challenged to identify themselves.

There are about fifty guests allowed to watch this ceremony, by invitation only. I do believe you have to ask for this invitation.

The Ceremony of the keys is held at two locations in the United Kingdom. The first at the Tower of London, the second in Edinburgh Castle. This nightly ritual is open for visitors by ticket admission only. There is no cost for the tickets. However, the tickets must be applied for in advance.

The Tower is closed for general admission and then locked at each entrance. These groups of people holding tickets are invited in. One of the best known Ceremonies is the one that takes place right here in England every night at the Tower of London.

No photography is allowed; the Yeoman Wardens perform their nightly ritual and pass along the keys.

The ceremony is completely silent except for the dialogue between Guards.

The ceremony The Sentry challenges the Keys.

Sentry: Who comes there?

Chief Warder: The Keys.

Sentry: Whose Keys?

Chief Warder: Queen Elizabeth's keys. (Identifying the keys as being those of the current British Monarch)

Sentry: Pass Queen Elizabeth's Keys, and all's well!

Following this, the party makes its way through the Bloody Tower Archway into the fortress, where they halt at the bottom of the Broad Walk Steps. On the top of the Stairs, under the command of their Officer, the Tower Guard present arms and the Chief Warder raises his hat, proclaiming:

Chief Warder: *God preserve Queen Elizabeth.*
Sentry and Tower Guard: *Amen!* (The Drummer sounds Last Post)

He then takes the keys to the Queen's House for safekeeping,

I did hear of a Guardsman on Duty during this Ceremony, and when he challenged the keys this is how it went, Sentry: Who comes there? Chief Warder: the keys: Sentry: Who's Keys? Chief Warder: Queen Elizabeth's Keys: Sentry; What the Fxxx are you doing with them then:

And as the saying go's it was in front of these entire guests' Needless to say he was rushed away and locked up. He probably got quite a few days nick.

Tower of London: complyments London-GB.com & Beefeater. London-GB.com.

Chapter (11)

The presentation of Colours to the Second Battalion Grenadier Guards, By Her Majesty the Queen.
1969.

THE NEW QUEEN'S COLOUR   THE NEW REGIMENTAL COLOUR

L/Cpl Gerald Griffiths and L/Sgt Southern on the left of the photo in the grounds of Buckingham Palace for the presentation of the Second Battalion Colours, 1969.

THE FIRST OR GRENADIER REGIMENT OF FOOT GUARDS

Presentation of Colours

to the

Second Battalion

by

HER MAJESTY THE QUEEN

Colonel-in-Chief of the Regiment

BUCKINGHAM PALACE
25th JUNE, 1969

Tangier, 1680
Namur, 1695
Gibraltar, 1704-5
Blenheim
Ramillies
Oudenarde
Malplaquet
Dettingen
Lincelles
Egmont-op-Zee
Corunna
Barrosa
Nive
Peninsular
Waterloo
Alma
Inkerman
Sevastopol
Tel-el-Kebir
Egypt, 1882
Suakin, 1885
Khartoum

Modder River
South Africa, 1899-1902
Marne, 1914
Aisne, 1914
Ypres, 1914, '17
Loos
Somme, 1916, '18
Cambrai, 1917, '18
Arras, 1918
Hazebrouck
Hindenburg Line
France and Flanders, 1914-18
Dunkirk, 1940
Mont Pincon
Nijmegen
Rhine
Mareth
Medjez Plain
Salerno
Monte Camino
Anzio
Gothic Line

THE FIRST OR GRENADIER REGIMENT OF FOOT GUARDS

Colonel-in-Chief:
HER MAJESTY THE QUEEN

Colonel:
MAJOR-GENERAL SIR ALLAN ADAIR, Bt.,
K.C.V.O., C.B., D.S.O., M.C., D.L., J.P.

Lieutenant-Colonel:
COLONEL A. N. BREITMEYER

Regimental Adjutant:
MAJOR D. H. C. GORDON LENNOX

Director of Music:
MAJOR R. B. BASHFORD, L.R.A.M., A.R.C.M.

Superintending Clerk:
SUPERINTENDING CLERK T. H. ASTILL

2nd BATTALION GRENADIER GUARDS

Commanding Officer:
LIEUTENANT-COLONEL P. H. HASLETT, M.B.E.

Second-in-Command:
MAJOR A. B. N. USSHER

Adjutant:
CAPTAIN J. BASKERVYLE-GLEGG

Quartermasters:
CAPTAIN A. DOBSON M.B.E.
LIEUTENANT T. PUGH

Regimental Sergeant-Major   R.S.M. R. HUGGINS
Drum Major   Drum Major R. TRUSSLER

Majors for Handing New Colours to Her Majesty The Queen:
Senior Major   MAJOR A. B. N. USSHER
Junior Major   MAJOR P. A. J. WRIGHT

Officers for the Colours:

Old:
2/LIEUT. C. S. S. LINDSAY
2/LIEUT. J. F. M. RODWELL

New:
2/LIEUT. A. C. ROUPELL
2/LIEUT. P. R. HOLCROFT

W.O. in charge of Old Colours   .. R.Q.M.S. A. ROBINSON
W.O.'s in charge of New Colours   .. D/Sgt. J. STANYARD
       A/D/Sgt. J. FORD

No. 1 COMPANY

MAJOR A. HEROYS
CAPTAIN THE MASTER OF ROLLO
2/LIEUT. C. G. HARRISS
C.S.M. D. PRITTY

No. 2 COMPANY

CAPTAIN P. M. L. SMITH
CAPTAIN A. J. C. WOODROW
LIEUT. P. J. S. HUSKINSON
C.S.M. B. EASTWOOD

SUPPORT COMPANY

MAJOR P. A. J. WRIGHT
CAPTAIN H. A. BAILLIE
LIEUT. H. J. LOCKHART
C.S.M. E. MITCHELL

THE INKERMAN COMPANY

MAJOR C. J. AIRY
CAPTAIN J. G. L. PUGH
2/LIEUT. C. P. KEYSER
C.S.M. J. FINNIS

THE ROYAL ARMY CHAPLAINS' DEPARTMENT

THE VENERABLE ARCHDEACON J. R. YOUENS, O.B.E., M.C., Q.H.C.,
Chaplain-General to the Forces.

THE REVEREND D. H. WHITEFORD, Q.H.C., M.A., B.D., Ph.D.,
Deputy Chaplain-General to the Forces.

THE REVEREND S. J. DAVIES, M.B.E., M.A.,
Chaplain to the Household Division.

THE RT. REVEREND MONSEIGNEUR J. O'SULLIVAN, M.B.E., V.G.
Principal RC Chaplain.

Deployment to Ireland, in 1969.

Throughout the years most wars have been about religion. Whether it is about the problems of today in Afghanistan or Iraq, be it Islamic, Catholic's, or Protestants or even the Inquisition of the early Century's, or even the Holy Wars, which lasted nearly two hundred years from 1095, through to 1272. The Third Crusade's leaving King Richard 1st to fight the remaining battles.

In 1969 and over the years in Ireland, it has all been about Catholic and Protestants. This goes back to even before the days of Oliver Cromwell in 1649. Some of the Conquests were from Anglo Norman. The King of Munster, Brain Boru was killed at the Battle of Clontarf in 1014. Before this Ireland was ruled from a system of small Kingdoms until the domination of King Henry 11 in 1171 and by 1175, which was the War of the Roses, until he had the control of Ireland. In 1541 King Henry V111 was declared the King of Ireland by the Irish Parliament, and the fighting over the right to vote for Parliament. But the fighting continued over these rights for a vote for the Parliament of Ireland and has continued until the present day.

Shortly after we returned from Germany in 1969 the Second Battalion Grenadier Guards was placed on 'Standby,' which wasn't supposed to be for long, and were stationed at Chelsea Barracks, then Commanded by Lieutenant Colonel Philip Hasslett. When the troubles started, Ian Paisley Protestant, and Bernadette Devlin Catholic, were at each other's throats and rioting in the streets soon broke out against these two factions.

As these troubles escalated, the Battalion was placed at very short notice on 'Standby' then days later 'Spearhead,' which means they could be sent to any trouble spot in the world at a moment's notice. Within a very short time the Battalion Spearheaded off to Londonderry in Northern Ireland, and based at Magilligan Point near the mouth of the River Foyle, while other Company's were placed at different locations including Belfast, Limavady as well as Londonderry to help contain the troubles.

The Inkerman Company was first deployed on the streets of Londonderry almost immediately to help contain these riots, which by now had broken out and had spilled onto the streets.

A small security Road Block and The Inkerman Company in Ireland.

The Inkerman Company 1961.

When the Second Battalion Grenadier's first deployed to Northern Ireland in 1969, I had around four or five months left to do in the army, and had to attend some resettlement course's for a job in civilian life, ready for my demob, and was kept back on the Rear Party, to help look after the Barracks.

Chapter (12)
Demobbed and Back into Civilian life.

After my demob, and during the following year, I had not quite got over rehabilitation into civilian life, and was finding it hard to settle down. I was still on reserve and pining to go back in the Army and talked to my wife about this, who then agreed to let me Re-enlist. I had actually gone through the procedure for this, and on the Thursday I received a letter to say, report to Pirbright when you can.

I had intended to collect my Railway Warrant on the Saturday at the Recruiting Office in Gloucester. However, on Friday I was talking to some of my mates that were Recruiting in Gloucester, who informed me we would be off to Germany again, and when the Married Quarters there were sorted out, we would be off to Northern Ireland again.

I was quite happy to except that, but the following day when I opened the papers the front page headline news was about two soldiers that had been lured out of a pub by two girls, and were murdered, shot in the back of the head by the I.R.A. (These two soldiers were the first to die by the hands of the I.R.A)
After this I had a lot of pressure not to go back in from June. My son was only three years old and growing fast. I would be away from them for some time, so decided not to go and decided to work harder on my Civilian life.

My first job was working for Lister's Engineering firm in Durlsey, Gloucestershire, which built Marine and power Generator Engines. I used to deliver these around the country in a three tonne truck. Later, as I was not able to stay away at night due to June's health I was able to get a Job on their Assembly Line, actually building them. It was a great job and I took to it like a Duck to Water.

Around 1972, I heard a Karate club was starting up in North Nibley, and several of my workmates plus myself went along. I thought it would be a good idea as I was getting unfit having driven trucks and sitting in their cabs all day. Not only that, but after years in the army I also thought it would feel good to get back into Unarmed Combat, especially after some of the practices I'd had with Karate in Germany and Kung Fu with the Chinese people in Guyana.

This was the start of my Martial Arts in a big way, and was now doing something I really enjoyed, which also helped me settle into Civilian life.

My own standards of fitness became rather high, and would push myself way above the limits of the average person, and think this was due to my competitive spirit during my army days. There was another student, Mike Peacock, who was a great one for competitiveness, and together would try to outdo each other, as well as push ourselves to the limit.

The Instructor at the Club was a man named Des Skilern, who was not only a good Instructor, but a great organiser at this rather large Club. Sadly, Des decided to start another Club and eventually left, leaving me to run the Club, which I successfully did for several years.

I then moved to Quedgeley in Gloucester, and began running Clubs in Gloucester, which is where until recently I trained and instructed.
You could read more on this subject in another book as part of a set, plus my teachings and philosophy of Martial Arts, along with my practices within Shoto's traditional Karate Kai, and hope I'm able to impress you?

Getting away from Martial Arts, I'd like to tell you a little more of where my life had led me.
I eventually left Listers, as I'd managed to secure a position with British Waterways. I was hoping to take over my father's Bridgeman's job at Slimbridge as I knew he'd soon be retiring, and thought it best to be working for them when this position finally became vacant.

I had secured a position of Piler, palletising the banks along the canal as Engineer, and sadly did not get my Dad's old job. That went to someone that had worked on the waterways for years, but they did offer me a bridge named, Simms Bridge, in Simms Lane.
So, we were living in Quedgeley, and living in a Waterways House working on Simms Bridge and was there for a couple of years.

Graham our son was now growing fast, he started doing the Martial Arts with me and at his age was beginning to get very good at it.

I also had a small cruiser which I had moored at my Mum and Dad's in Slimbridge.

We had it up on the bank, for a while, when doing work on it.

This is a photo with my son Graham standing in front of it.

We named it The Grenadier.

Graham about eleven.
With Mum and Dad.

Grahams first School Photo

Then, in 1977 the Rea Bridge, which is the next bridge down from Simms Bridge became vacant, and I managed to get that position, and that is where we remained until recent.

We actually moved during the Christmas Holiday, we were going along the Canal Bank even on Christmas Day! Backwards and forwards along that canal bank, which seemed endless, but both bridges are in sight of each other as can be seen in these two photos, the Simms Bridge being the one in the distance.

At the time I had no car, so everything had to be carefully piled into my wheelbarrow and moved, which was a hard slog, but we manages to do it!

'Oh', how about that! The swan was attacking the rowers as they went by.

My Dad was very happy for us, and glad I managed to get this Bridge, and always said he was sure we would be happy there. Dad was a great guy and well liked by everyone who knew him. Knowing and seeing the Bridge that I had, he said you should have some wonderful times here, just like he had at Slimbridge.

My Dad said, 'Wow! You won't have to open it as many times as I used to,' as the Rea Bridge was so much higher from the water than the one he worked, and most boats could safely pass underneath its span.

Chapter (13).

On 24th October 1978 my father died. His death, although we knew it could happen, hit the family hard. He'd had Pneumonia a couple of years earlier, which left him with a weak heart, and because of this, had a pacemaker fitted.

Mum used to joke about this by saying: If she wanted sex, she would have to plug him into the mains! To which Dad would reply: that although the pacemaker was small, his arms got tired carrying a twelve volt car battery around all day. Which goes to show his sense of humour?

This was an extremely sad time, especially as it was our father and the first close member of our family we'd lost, and all his son's, including myself, were pallbearers at his funeral and carried his coffin.

As we came out of the church all the birds started chirping, and a similar thing happened a few years later at Mum's funeral. I remember holding back the tears as we slowly walked him to the graveside, and started shaking. My brother Christopher, who was my partner on the coffin, gently squeezed my arm to tell me to hold myself together, and pulling my head up, managed to carry on in a proudly and dignified way.

This is my Dad, June, and I, with Mum and a family friend, walking along the Canal bank in 1978.

This is Dad in topper hat, with Mum at happy times in Slimbridge and David selling stuff at his stall.

Chapter (14)

Sadly, on 11ᵗʰ April 1991 my sister Mary passed away. We were on holiday in Australia at the time, and when we returned my dear sister did not have long to live. All the family rallied around, including my sister living in Australia, who we'd recently said goodbye to, which because of a stopover in Singapore on our way home, had actually arrived home before we did!
The morning after we arrived home, she rang us. I thought she was ringing from Australia to see if we'd arrived home safely, but she was actually at the hospital with Mary! So we left at once to be with them both.
My dear brother Peter also came home from Australia to be with her before she passed on, and we were all able to say our goodbyes.

She was a very courageous Lady, and showed great sereneness in her last moments. I would like to acknowledge the wonderful way my other baby Sister Angela looked after Mary, and nursed her, and was there at Mary's every beck and call, right up to the very end. Angela was everybody's rock.

Three of Mary's Grandchildren, at her graveside in 2011. Left to right: Morgan, Cora, Shinead. Mary never got to see any of her Grandchildren.

Mary about 10 years old, fifteen and sixteen.

Looking back on some of the finest memories of Mary. Mary would do anything for anyone, she was kind and generous, and had two lovely daughters Vicky and Sarah.

It was such a shame as her daughter, Vicky was pregnant at the time, and did not get to see her first grandchild.
I remember going to a party for our David and wife Janet. I believe it was their fiftieth Anniversary and took Mary and Mum in my car. While the party was in full swing, Ian, David's Son in Law, tried to get Mary drunk. Mary was drinking Brandy, while Ian was drinking Pints. Anyway, as the evening wore on Mary still looked sober, while Ian was as the proverbial Newt! Mary was still holding good conversation, as a Lady would, and did not look at all drunk.

Well, when we got back to the car Mary plonked herself down on the back seat and said, 'Oh my God! I'm so pissed, that bloody Ian!' and that was the only time she looked drunk. A Lady to the end!

Mary and I used to love to dance, and think we inherited this from Dad, especially as he was a fine dancer. We also loved to Jive, as in 'Rock and Roll' and done this really fast. Other dancers would often stop and watch us on the floor, and on many occasions gave us a standing ovation! 'Cool or what?'
These next few pages are dedicated to Mary. She will live in our hearts forever

A lovely photos of a very young Mary and Angela.

Mary and Jeff's wedding.

Mary with Baby Sarah.

Mary with Glenis and Peter, Peter came from Australia to see her.

This is a photo of Mary, I've had it in my wallet since my birthday in 1962.

It was taken in a photo-booth when Mary came down to see me at the Cenotaph as a weeping sentry in Bristol all those years ago.

Molly and June. Molly & Bob are friends of Mum from America, Mum Mary and Me.

At Mary's funeral, there was standing room only. The church was packed, and some people had to stand outside. The florist in Cam and Dursley ran out of flowers, this show's what a popular girl she was. Later that year, I managed to hold a Memorial Dance in her memory, at Lister's Hall in Dursley.

It was in aid of Cancer, the money to go to the Cobalt Unit, ward 10, in Cheltenham. The tickets were a sell-out. All her friends and relatives were there, and were all talking about Mary and some of the funny and good times they all had.

On the night of the dance we held a prize draw, which was to contribute to the fund for the Cancer Cobalt Unit. There were some very funny instances. One prize was where someone won some hair conditioner, though they themselves were bold.
Another was, where someone won a tray of meat, even though they were Vegetarians. Another prize was when someone won a bottle of Brandy and they were a recovering alcoholic.

We are sure Mary was looking down and picked out these prizes for a laugh.
We did have a good laugh about it too.

Gerald with the Head Nurse, Cobalt Unit, ward 10 Cheltenham.

Several Nurses came to the dance From the Cobalt Unit.

After the dance we tallied the money up after paying for the band and billed for the hall, it came to a grand total of £777-00.

Which was presented to the Cobalt Unit a few weeks later.

This is June and I with my Mum at Cheltenham. Presenting the Cheque to the two head nurses from the Unit in the Ward 10.

These are the nurses which cared for Mary. Our thanks go to them for everything they did for her.

Marys second Marriage just a few years before she died.
With Myself and three Brother's, Graham, David and Chris.

Magic moments at wedding

By ANDREA GARDINER

LOCAL bride Mary Boyle had the greatest surprise of her life when she appeared in the doorway of St Bartholomew's Church, Cam, after taking her vows — from behind one of the many cameras that eagerly pointed in her direction popped the head of her sister Sheila Waller, who had unexpectedly travelled all the way from 'down under' to witness the occasion.

Sheila, who had assured her sister that she could not attend the wedding two weeks ago, hid in the vestry until the service began, before creeping to the back of the church to secretly view the ceremony.

Having luckily escaped relatives' attention, she then crept outside to witness one of the most dramatic exits from church a bride has ever made.

Mary leapt from her elegant bridal stance and jumped up and down for joy. Overwhelmed relatives watched as the two sisters hugged and kissed each other.

Nobody at the wedding knew of Sheila's arrival in England, as she had stayed with friends in Bristol until the morning of the wedding.

Proud mother Mrs E M Griffiths (75), of Tyndale Road, Woodfields, Cam, had received a subtle warning from the vicar, the Rev Cecil Alway, that she may be in for a shock after the service.

But the appearance of her distant daughter could not have been further from her mind.

She said: 'It was one of the best days of my life. I do not think I will ever recover from the shock. I am on cloud nine.

'Mary had already had a pleasant surprise on the night before her wedding when Sheila phoned to wish her good luck.

'We thought she was phoning from Australia but it turns out that she was calling from Bristol.'

Sheila (50) emigrated to Australia 27 years ago with her husband who owns a laundry business in Sydney. Plans to come to England were only finalised two weeks before the wedding, and Sheila had to brave the 30-hour flight alone.

But she declared: 'It was worth every minute. When Mary appeared through the doors of the church, it was a magic moment that I would not have missed for the world.'

Mary and her new husband Mr Stephen Boyle were followed by tearful relatives to the reception at The Berkeley Vale Hotel, Stone, where they enjoyed a buffet and entertainment by live bands.

The following morning the happy couple left for a honeymoon in Anglesey where they hoped to recover from the shock.

But the celebrations continued throughout the week at the home of Mrs Griffiths where Sheila is staying for the rest of her four-week visit.

Mrs Griffiths, who boasts of nine wonderful children, has two more sons and a daughter in Australia, but unfortunately they could not make the occasion.

She said: 'I have been to Australia many times and my family have visited me, but nothing could match this unforgettable surprise.'

The newly-weds are going to live in Severn Road, Cam, where they hope to be visited many more times by their thoughtful sister.

DURSLEY 2931   July 28 1989

• Mrs E M Griffiths and her daughter Sheila who provided extra 'magic moments' at her sister Mary's wedding when she unexpectedly appeared from 'down under'. (89/1329)

Thanks to the Dursley Gazette for this story

This is an old picture, Mary had gone over to Stroud to Uncle Ernie's and went out for the day with John Griffiths, her Cousin they just got back from a cyicle ride.

'God bless you Mary, 'I Love you'.

Chapter (15)

This is a great photo of Peter's family. I took this when June and I stayed at Peter's Home at Black Butt in Queensland.

In October 1991 Peter came home from Australia to be with Mary, and while he was here visited most of the family, but of course spent the greater part of his time with Mary. Here are some great pictures of him starting with his family in Australia, plus a photo of him when he was a young 'Super Star!'

Laura.   Aaron.   Jesse.   And Amy.

This is a picture of Peter in his singing 'Super Star' days during the Sixties and Seventies.
I can remember coming home on leave from the army and seeing him singing with his Band, I was so proud of him, 'he was great', I was telling everyone, 'hey, he's my brother.
'I love him dearly.'

Peter and Shirley's Children.    And Peter outside Mums.

Peter & Gerald visiting our Christopher and Penny.

With Mum in her garden and with his best mate,
Colin Alan, who passed away only a few years ago.

Peter, Mo and Family.   Peter with a mate John Keedwell.   Peter & Mum cooking.

Mum & Peter.   Peter, Julie and Janet.   Angela & Peter.

Love you; Peter and Shirley. 2010.

Chapter (16)

Back to the Rea Bridge and my life.

In 1980 I took redundancy, and basically retired for a few years. During this time June and I went travelling, and had a couple of holidays.

But, the big thing was, Waterways sold the house to June and I. We have had so many memories there, and some great Garden Parties. One of these was when my neighbour, Norman Broady surprised us by having Jet Harris from the Shadows and his Band play in our garden, it was a fantastic surprise. Norman was an Entertainments Agent, and had great influence throughout the entertainments world, he was a wonderful generous man. We used to have fantastic times at Norman and Margaret's house, the jamming, singing and Karaoke sessions were absolutely great.

This is a picture about 1978 with my dog. Our house in the background.

June, Gerald and Jet Harris from the Shadows, in our garden.

Shadows star livens up the party.

FORMER Shadows star Jet Harris was a welcome gatecrasher at a neighbour's party in Gloucester.

Jet, former bass player with the Shadows and once a million-selling pop star, turned up univited at the party in Elmore Lane, Quedegley — and asked host, Mr. Gerald Griffiths where his band could plug in their equipment.

"I thought he was joking," said Mr. Griffiths. "But they weren't — they entertained us for the whole afternoon and evening and it was fantastic."

And for Mr. Griffiths, who was holding a skittles and social evening in the back garden of his house in aid of charity, Jet's arrival was a stroke of luck.

Mr. Griffiths, of Rea Bridge House, explained: "I had booked a disco but they didn't turn up. I didn't really know this at the time, but my next door neighbour, Mr. Norman Broady, who works for the Gloucester Entertainments Agency, booking acts, turned up in my garden all of a sudden with Jet Harris.

"In fact the whole band, Jet Harris and the Strangers, turned up."

Mr. Griffiths said he had met Jet, who lives a few doors up from him in Elmore Lane, a couple of times before. "But I'm getting to know him well now. He's a really pleasant guy — terrific!"

Jet, who found fame and fortune with the Shadows and lost it again, has now settled down to a quieter life in Gloucestershire where he can indulge his photography skills.

But he is still remembered for his hits with the Shadows, who backed Cliff Richard, and his massive-selling record "Diamond" which he recorded in the 1960s with drummer Tony Meehan.

Reeling

Mr. Griffiths said: "It was absolutely fantastic to have him there. They were so kind to just turn up out of the blue like that. I'm still reeling from the shock," he said.

And while Jet and the Strangers were making music, Mr. Griffiths was taking the opportunity to get to grips with a hair-raising problem — shaving off his beard in aid of charity.

The evening was in aid of Quedgeley Karate Club, where Mr. Griffiths is an instructor, and kidney research.

The evening raised £60

Press cutting thanks to the Gloucester Citizen.

Norman Broady, Jet Harris and Margret Broady.

A party in full swing. Greta a friend, Mum and Glenis, my Sister in Law.

Picture of the Rea Bridge House, taken from the Bridge.

A wonderful, Sunset, that was taken from the Bridge.
We can see these from our living room window.
These sunsets I have taken, are only a fraction of what I have been able to take.

This is my stunningly beautiful wife June on her fiftieth birthday.

This is Gerald on his fiftieth birthday.

This was our twenty fifth Wedding Anniversary.
We renewed our wedding vows at Quedgeley Church, on 18th December 1982.

This is at the reception in the Golden Dragon, in Gloucester. No I am not going to pour it over her. A picture of my great looking wife June, we are just going to a dance.

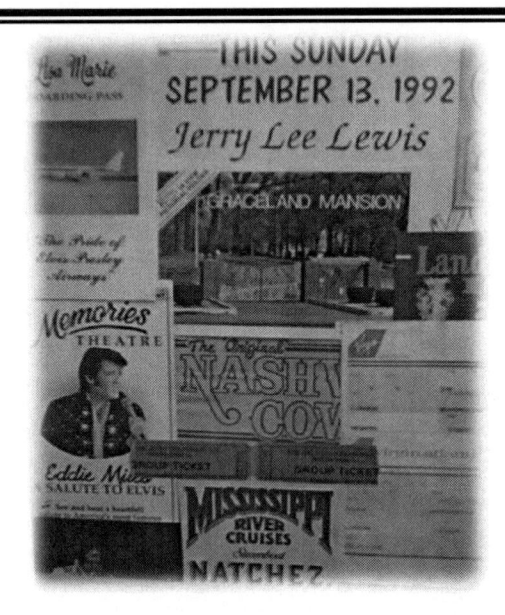

This is a collage taken in two parts, and hangs in our hallway with some of the photos taken on the trip. When Norman and Margaret moved in next door, we became very close, more like family than friends and love them dearly, we had some wonderful times together.

We also went on a fantastic holiday to America with them, and what a wonderful time it was. It was a tour of America with a musical theme. We started off in New York, Washington, Delaware, Rownox, Knoxville, Nashville, Tennessee, Mississippi, New Orleans, Memphis, Tallahassee, Orland, Miami back home. It was a trip of a lifetime, and that was all done in a fortnight, we did not even have time to be tired. But when we got back from it we must have slept for weeks.

This is a Bar in down town Nashville.

In a shop for clothes in Nashville.

This coat was made of Doeskin.

Gerald singing in the auditorium of the Grand Ole Opry.

The Sun Recording Studio's. This is where Elvis made his first record.
'That's all right Mama.'
You obviously gather we like Elvis, we do, but not fanatical about him,
it was all part of the tour.

June at Graceland's. This cross is next to Elvis's grave.

May Elvis rest in peace?

Gerald and June, by the statue of Elvis, down town Memphis.

This was a square dancing club.

This is the Cafe, where Elvis signed up with Edd Parker.

Outside the door of Graceland's.

Our hotel, down town Memphis.

June, outside the Peabody Hotel.

This hotel has about a dozen Mallard Ducks that live there. Every morning they come down in the lift to go to the pond in the foyer for the day, where all the guest's can feed them, then at dusk they wait at the lift to go back to the roof of the Penthouse to roost. When they go up or down, the hotel plays some music, which is called the march of the Peabody Ducks. This happens every day of the year, and is quite famous, people stand each side of the foyer to watch and take photos as they March towards the font and fountain in the foyer.

During our time in Memphis, we were given a choice. We could go down town, or look at famous people's houses, we thought, 'Boring' and chose to go to a bar in down town as it would be nicer. It did turn out to be nice in the bars, and we did meet some really nice people.

But! When we got back, the people from the coach party said they had seen Johnny Cash's house and Jim Reeves house, and while they were looking at his house Mrs Reeve's came out to the gate and invited them all in for tea! Yes! They were all invited in by Mrs Reeve's and had tea in her parlour and saw his Gold Records on the wall! They said it was wonderful, and what a privilege! Afterwards, Norman was forever pulling my leg about this as he knew I liked Jim Reeve's.

The Peabody Ducks, waddling down the red carpet.

While we were in New Orleans, we stayed in the French Quarter in the Bourbon Hotel on the corner of Bourbon Street. This is the horse drawn carriage that took us around the City of New Orleans. Gerald up the front then June and Norman, and behind Norman, is Margaret and two of our friends we met on the coach party. ----------------------------------

This horse drawn carriage took us around the city, we then went to the docks to go on a fantastic cruse down the Mississippi River on one of the New Orleans Paddle Steamers. It was huge, and made a three point turn, just to turn around on a river like the Mississippi, that's nearly 4 Mile's wide! The Paddle Steamer was so long in length. There were three dance bands playing at once in the same Ballroom, and each one was out of ear shot of the other. The Buffet Table was so long you would not believe it.

New Orleans night life is amazing, especially around the French Quarter. Every other building is a Bar or Nightclub with a shop in between, which sells everything from cans of beans to Sex Toys of one sort or another.

We were sitting in our hotel having our evening meal, which was on the ground floor, next to an open window, and overlooked the main Bourbon Street.

The opposite building was a Nightclub, and in the wall above the door were two round holes, and just as I said to June, I wonder what those are for, two naked legs appeared and began going in and out of these holes! This turned out to be a naked stripper the other side of the wall on a swing!

Then a big fat naked stripper came out onto the street to try and lure passersby into their club! That was the last thing I wanted to see while having Dinner. But the food was amazing.

A pub in Orlando. Look at the height of this Bear!

Gerald in a bar in Orlando.

Jerry Lee Lewis, the Rock and Roll singer in down town Memphis Tennessee, we were sitting right at this table only a few feet away. He was brilliant.

June & Gerald, with Margret & Norman in Nashville Tennessee.

June sitting by Elvis's pool behind his grave.   Elvis statue down town Memphis.

Well, we are now back home and took weeks to get over the holiday, but we had such a wonderful time.

From the time Margret and Norman moved next door to us, we have had some wonderful exciting times, and will always recognise and remember, that our lives would never have been the same if they had not done so.

This is a painting, I painted thirty years ago, which was sold for charity.
Someone in Bristol had bought it for around thirty pounds.
I called it: Elvis at the Pearly Gates'.

Christmas over Margret & Norman's.

Sadly Norman Died on 18th July 2002. We will miss him so much, and was one of the nicest people you could ever wish to meet. His sense of humour was great as well, and was a subtle type of humour. One night we were at a Country and Western party. Norman had gone to the toilet, and when he came back he said there was an Indian Chief in there who was trying to have a tee-pee, but he could not go because he was two tents, 'that was his sense and sort of humour'. We loved him dearly.

Christmas over Margret and Norman's around 1980. In this picture is my Mum with Margret.

Left to right: June, Graham and Sharon. Left to right: Graham, Norman, Sharon and Robert.

This is a Wishing Well, and Bar-B-Q I built for Margret & Norman, about twenty five years ago and they are both still there to this very day.

This is my garden. I made the Barbeque and the bird table.
Earlier in the book, I told you about the time when June came to join me when I was posted to Germany with the Guards, and had bought her some presents for when she got there. One of the presents was some LP's of Frank Ifield. Well, I was out opening the bridge during my job on Waterways and saw a Gold Rolls Royce outside Margaret's and Norman's house. I could not resist going in to find out who was there.

To my surprise it was Frank Ifield. It was great to have met him. I asked if it was alright for me to bring June over to meet him. He was so kind and really did not mind at all, a really nice man.
When I got back home, all I said to June was Margaret wanted to borrow her Frank Ifield Records, would she take them over. What a great surprise for June when she met him, it was wonderful. She shook his hand and he kisses her on the cheek, and she was so cool about it and thanked him, he also signed June's L.P's.
We then said our goodbyes and left. When June got a safe distance from the house she danced a Jig and was jumping up and down saying, 'I've just met Frank Ifield!' She was over the moon!
Australian Singer/Songwriter and Yodeller Frank Ifield, was one of the more original country artists to come from overseas. He was born in England, and moved to Australia in 1948. While still in his teens, he became a regular on Bonnington's Bunkhouse, a popular radio program, and dropped out of school to pursue a music career full-time. He appeared on other radio shows as well, finally landing on the travelling Ted Quigg Show, where he stayed for many years.

Ifield signed with EMI Australia in 1953 and released two successful singles including 'There's a Love knot in My Lariat.' Soon he was hosting a weekly television show Campfire Favourites. By 1959, Ifield was appearing on all three of the Sydney Television Channels. Later that year, he went to London, and had his first British hit in 1960 with 'Lucky Devil.' He remained in England and in 1962 became a star with his yodeling classic 'I remember you.' The song stayed at the top of the British charts for over two months, and when released in the States, hit number five on the pop charts. His most successful year was 1963 when he scored two British number one hits, one of those being, 'I'm Confessin (That I Love you.)

He continued having pop chart success through 1964, but after that his career in Britain began to wane. He went to Nashville in 1966 and was made an Honorary Tennessean by the State's Governor Frank Clement. Ifield recorded two albums in Nashville and debuted on the Grand Ole Opry, where he was a great success.

During 1966-67, he had several mid-range hits, 'Call Her Your Sweetheart, No One will ever know,' and 'Tale of Two Cities,' recorded for *Hickory*. He again found popularity in Europe during the 70's, particularly in Belgium, Holland and Luxembourg, and continued to tour and perform at country music festivals and cabarets. ~ Sandra Brennan, All Music Guide.

Meeting celebrities was always happening at Margaret's and Normans. They were coming and going all the time. I've jammed with Kenny Ball and his Jazz-Band, and sung with Jet Harris with him playing his guitar.
In fact it was Jet Harris who said that I could sing and should practice, as he thought I could do well at it. We used to have great singing sessions, and had so much fun over there. Margaret, June and I used to write down all the words to songs and would be singing along to tapes, so in a way, we were the first ones to be doing Karaoke.
One Day David Butler from the television program 'The Comedians' was over there, and I found out that he use to go to school with my two brothers Graham and David, which was the same Secondary School I attended in Wick Road!

Also I am a singer and karaoke presenter, and as you can see I enjoy Country and Western.
I Like Elvis and 'Rock and Roll.' I have been on X-Factor and passed two additions.
I enjoyed singing and feel or wish I could have got further with it.
But who known's? Someday I may give it another go!

Chapter (17)

Graham growing into a fine young man and his life.

Graham playing in Cam and with Gran and Suzy our Dog.

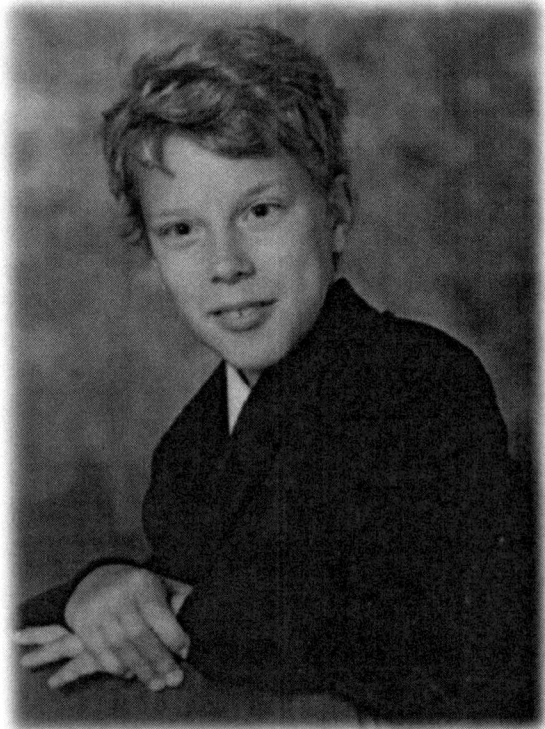

Graham about Seven years old, and eleven years old.

Graham at Eleven 1/2 This was the first year after we moved to Rea Bridge House in 1978.

Graham at twelve years old.   Severn Vale school photo at thirteen.

Graham with his Mum, at fifteen. Graham at sixteen, his first job after leaving school at Debenhams.

Graham coming up to eighteen and Graham's Eighteenth birthday party at the Golden Dragon in Gloucester.

Chapter (18)

Graham and Terese at their Marriage in Cheltenham August 1991.

In 1991, the same year Mary died, Graham returned from Australia. He had stayed there for a few months after we came home. When he arrived home, he had a young lady with him. It was not long after they decided to get married and tied the knot on August of that year 1991. Her name was Terese Fay and they lived in Cheltenham.

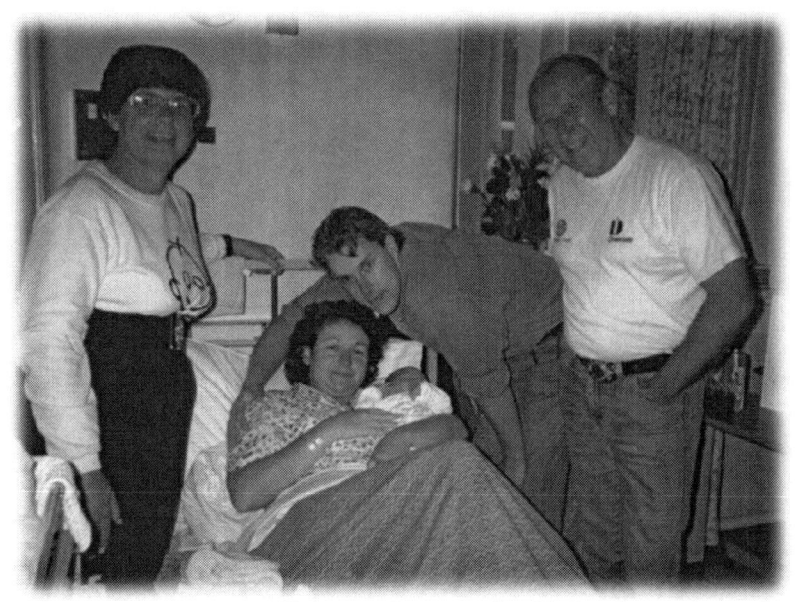

Just over a year later. Larrisa Fay Griffiths was born at the Cheltenham Maternity Hospital on the 3rd of July 1992. We were over the moon, she was so beautiful, our lovely Granddaughter.

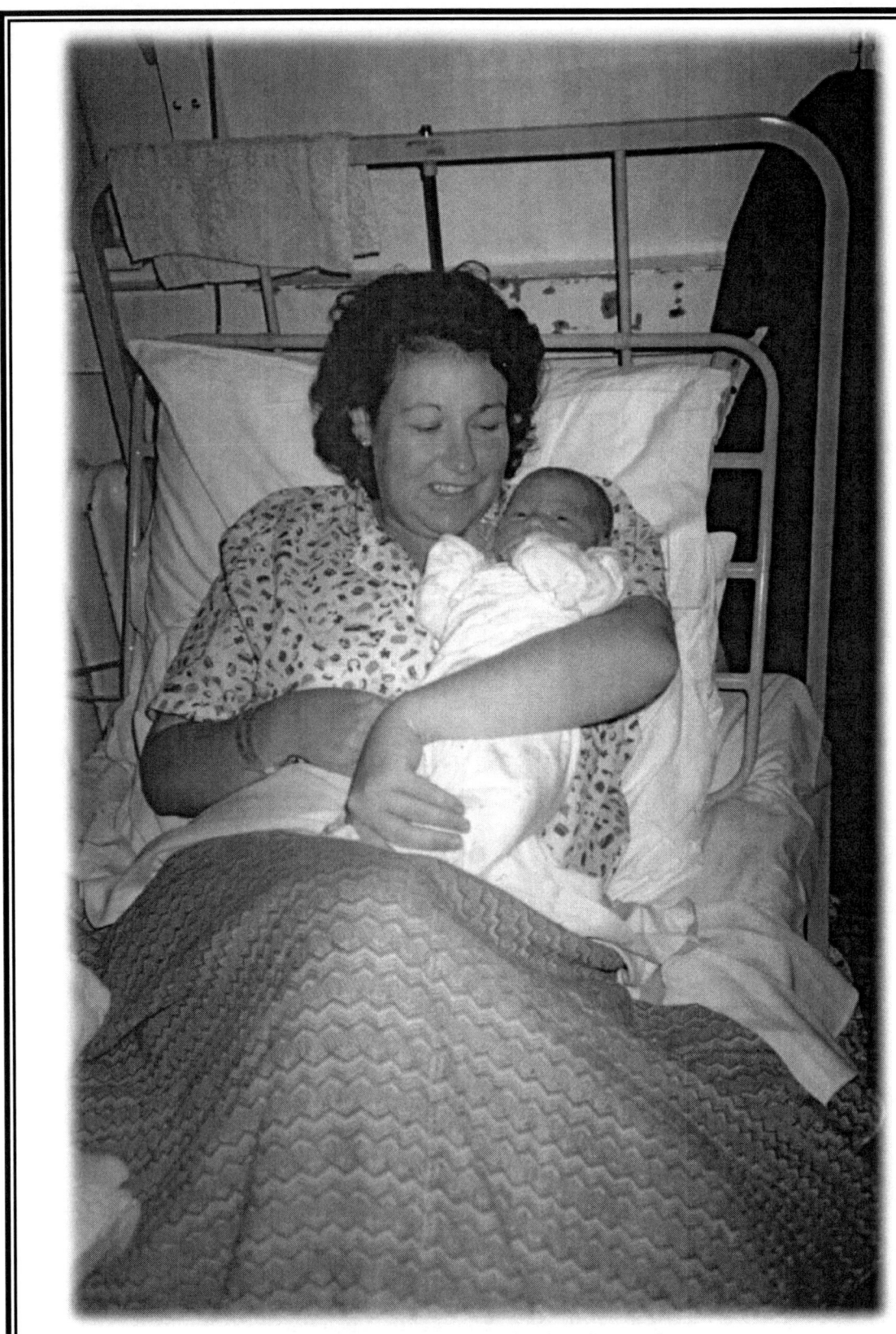

Terese and baby Larrisa, on the day she was born.

June (Mama), nursing baby Larrisa, born on the 3rd of July 1992.

We were so happy for Graham, as he was so happy. His lovely daughter was so beautiful, and Terese and Graham treasured her.

Graham almost the same age as Larrisa with both Mum's, as in the pictures.

Larrisa, a month old and Gran-(Mama) June.

Then five years later on the 11th June 1997 our Grandson was born. Graham and Terese named him Brandon, he was a great little chap and we were now such proud Grandparents of two lovely children. Larrisa is holding him here and she was so proud of him and loves him dearly just as much as his Mum and Dad.

Baby Brandon, Larrisa and Terese, their Mum.

A lovely day out with the Grandchildren in London.
Brandon looking through the gates at Buckingham Palace.

Larrisa, outside Buckingham Palace.

We had a great day with the children, showing them around London, and at Buckingham Palace. Larrisa said she loved Buckingham Palace, and said she would like to come back there again someday, when she was older.
I wonder if she remembers that?

Larrisa looking through the gates of Buckingham Palace.

Larrisa and June (Mama), outside Buckingham Palace.

Brandon, Great-Gran Griffiths, and Larrisa.

Brandon's school photo.

Granddad and Mama, on the helter-skelter, with Larrisa and Brandon.

That was fantastic fun but scary. We had taken Brandon and Larrisa to Lego Land near Windsor for the day before they went out to live in Australia. We had quite a few rides on different things and we tried to please them both by going on them, even though we were a little scared, (well June was!)
Brandon and Larrisa loved the rides and they seemed fearless, to all of them. It was so hard to keep up with them, but it was a wonderful day and we would not have missed it for the world, we just wanted them to be happy, especially as they were so close to going to Australia, to live.

Larrisa School Photo. Posing in a store.

Chapter (19). **It's four in the Morning.**

It's four in the morning, and I just can't sleep. Just thinking about my family, Grahams Marriage broke up, and split a while ago. We are all getting that much older, and do worry about some of my family members and if they're alright. I do worry about Graham and what he has been through these last few years, and of course his Crones' disease.

It's just that a member of the family was celebrating the anniversary of their Mum's death at the weekend, and said she was glad to have told her Mum how much she loved her. What with being so close to my own mother's death, and the loss of a dear sister, it brought it all flooding back. Maybe I have been bottling it up all this time, because I found it hard to sleep, and as I was laying there crying, I thought it best to get up. So, here I am rambling away and venting my feelings on the Computer Keyboard.

I do feel so much for my family, and wish I could take their pain away. I would also like them to know I love them dearly! Oh, Shit! Here I go again getting all emotional, and can hardly see the keyboard for tears!

Due to June's health we were only blessed with one child, our son Graham. We would love to have had more. But because we only have Graham, we treasure his love and respect all the more, and of course our two Grandchildren, which we love so much. I don't know what I would do if we were to lose their love Graham, Brandon, and Larrisa, I don't think I would be able, or want to live without them in my life.

June and I are missing them dreadfully as they now live in Australia, and have taken the decision to live there ourselves. We have chosen South Australia, because the cost of living is far better and can purchase a far better house in a much better Rural Seaside location. We do understand this will be a long way from the Grandchildren, but hopefully see a great deal more of them, than we do now.
I often think: 'Maybe they think we've let them down' by not doing enough for them. But we have always tried to be part of their lives as much as we could, and helped out financially wherever we could, even at the expense of going without ourselves.

To think, I am now a year older than I was when my father died, life can be so unfair. After what Dad went through during the War Years, the extreme weather conditions of the Arctic Convoys in the Barren Sea to Russia, and for Dad to die at the age of sixty seven after all those hardships, just doesn't seem fair! And now, in 2009, my mother has died! At least she had a good long life, and died peacefully in her sleep.

Larrisa.

Now they both have gone, there's a large hole in my life, but hold on to the fact I have a loving son and two beautiful Grandchildren, Larrisa and Brandon. As I witness my Grandchildren growing, I know Larrisa is destined for something special. She is such a special girl herself, and in the past, when she was growing up at Emu Park, what happened to her family moved me to realise just how special she was, and growing into a fine understanding person. I remember her confiding in me some of the things that was happening in her life.

She was so understanding and supportive, I think she was the person that kept Graham going, as well as keeping it together for his children. This was a hard time for them all, which is always the same at the breakup of any family or marriage where children are involved, and as time went on, things became difficult for them all.

Larrisa managed to stay firm and focus on her schooling at the School in Mt Larcom. I was as impressed and proud for her as she became Senior School Captain and organised the School Deb-Graduation on the 29th November 2007, at the Gladstone Leagues Club. How grown and beautiful she looked, giving out the speeches and awards for pupils and staff.

Larrisa was so popular at this school and had so many friends, of which we got to meet. Even now she is still in contact with many of them, come to that she is still in contact with lots of her old school friends in England; which she had before she went to Australia. I think this is more on her part, as she has such a loving nature, and likes to keep in contact.

Larrisa taken at her Graduation.

'Keep your dreams alive'. Understand to achieve anything requires faith and belief in yourself, vision, hard work, determination, and dedication. Remember all things are possible for those who believe.' I am sure that Larrisa believes in these things to.

Larrisa's Graduation, with some of her close friends.

Larrisa is always so popular; she is bubbly outgoing with a beautiful loving nature and has so many friends.

Her expression shows so much in this photo.

Larrisa, is always smart and looking beautiful and does like to dress up and party.

Brandon, Emu Park 2007 and Ipswich Brisbane 2010.

Obviously it was hard for Brandon as well. He was only eight years old during this time and living at Emu Park, at the breakup of Graham and Terese. He too was able to pull through it all with great strength and durability, which a child of his age could have at that time. We, as adults, don't give credit to the strength and adaptability of young children, as they seem to recover better than most adults through crisis like this. They can be more forgiving than adults where the unconditional love works both ways from Mother to child and Father to child, where unacquainted love can, and should always pull through for all the family. The break and separation was difficult, but Graham and Teresa kept it very amicable for the happiness of their children, with unconditional love of double access.

Due to the break up, Graham and the children had to move, and moved to Raglan on the Bruce Highway Nr' Gladstone, in 2006. At the time, Graham was desperate for the children to finish their term at school, so had to make do with the home he had taken, which was not adequate enough for them. 'A little bit run down'.

Brandon is a brilliant athlete, and has lots of determination to do well in all he does.

Brandon had his school's athletics while we were there, I watched him as he did so well, and won numerous races. It was a wonderful day meeting his friends and their families. Brandon was also very good on his BMX bike. I have seen him jumping with his bike in the BMX Park, and was very impressed with his ability. 'He was fantastic!' as you can see by these two photos, that's a big jump.

As you can see, Larrisa and Brandon love each other very dearly. I think these pictures were taken at Emu Park. We also fell in love with Emu Park, it was such a lovely place with a beautiful coastline. The nearest big town is Rockhampton, which was not too many miles away. It was not long after, Graham and his family moved to Raglan near Gladstone.

Gerald (Granddad) & June (MaMa) Larrisa and Brandon

at Gladstone Queensland.

Brandon & Larrisa.

Larrisa has grown into a beautiful young woman.

Larrisa at Eighteen years.

History repeating itself.

In 2008, I had come off the phone to Graham in Australia. After we talked for a while he said he had to go, as he is on the way to pick Larrisa up from work. She was working at MacDonald's, I thought this is certainty history repeating itself! God, the times I have sat outside MacDonald's myself, sometimes at one or two o'clock in the morning, waiting for Graham to finish work.

This was when he was about sixteen, the same age Larrisa is now in 2008.

I would be waiting hours only to find he had already left. This is love, and now twenty five years later he is doing just the same things as me. Now he probably knows why we worried about him!

I can remember when some men jumped him and his friend, but with Martial Arts Training and my strong influence on him, he handle it OK, and came away unhurt. I expect he now worries about Larrisa, probably more so being a young girl, and in a big city like Brisbane.

This would be about 1983 outside MacDonald's in Gloucester, where Graham worked.

Graham at Emu Park in Queensland 2006.

The Loves and the aspirations.

To your loved ones, from someone who cares.

When does a mother stop loving a child after bonding with it unconditionally from birth? More so with a mother than a father, as they have come from her very loins. How can these things happen? I will never know! This unconditional love a parent has, 'is for life', so if a child does wrong in their adult life, how do you cope with it? Are you going to extradite and disown them? Or do you forgive them and move on? The unrequited love starts at the very being of your life and soul with them, and should continue for your entire life here on earth. Don't let things go on too long. If you have fallen out with a member of your family, and you really love them. 'Talk and put things right'. No one should be above reconciliation, and it should be the responsibility of the older person of a dispute, to put it right.
I can never understand people who can look into the eyes of their baby with unconditional love, then when they become adults a father or a mother, can disown or stop speaking to their daughter or son because of a stupid argument, or for whatever reason. Where has that unconditional love gone that has become irretrievable, 'it is so sad'?

 The aspirations and love for your child, and love for your Grandchildren, haven't just been forgotten. I could never ever let that happen to me, I love my son so much, just like my parents loved me. When does the love for a brother or a sister stop, when they cannot speak to each other, for so long?

It's too late to say, 'I'm sorry' when they are in there grave, or show your love for them. You can only have this opportunity when they are alive. I will never let it happen to my immediate family, how can a brother and sister grow up together with bonding love for each other, then throw it all away through some misspoken words, and never speak to each other again. How can they do that?

 I love my son, my Granddaughter Larrisa, and Grandson Brandon so much, and missing them terribly, and can't wait to go to Australia to be with them.

 If you think these words can be associated with your own family life, and I have been able to touch your own conscience. Look into your heart, try and do something about it, phone, or meet and tell them you love them! Swallowing pride and forgiveness, even if you are right or wrong.

Do not forget that unconditional love that you first felt and saw as you bonded with your child, whether it is Son, Daughter, Brother or Sister, Mother or Father or whoever. Do it before it's too late, and tell them you love them!

'In talking things over'.

In talking things over you often find, -that the knots and tangles will unwind. In talking things over, it might well be, that a different viewpoint you will see. In talking things over you get a fresh light, on the whole situation, the wrong and the right. Thrashing it out in a friendly tone, is better than thinking it out alone. So don't go around with a harboured grudge. Don't take a side and refuse to budge, for there is no grievance that can't be healed, and there is no problem that will not yield. In talking things over. <u>A poem author unknown.</u>

Very close friendships.

If you have a friend, and have been friends for years and years, surely all those years can't just be thrown down the pan, just because something had been said that you disagreed with or something you disliked.

By putting pride and predigest aside, so you could at least talk to resolve a dispute or a dislike that you thought you had. A very long friendship doesn't come along very often, where a friend had stuck by you through thick and thin, especially a friendship where you have had some bad times, where your friend has been there for you.

It is also just as important in a long term friendships, as in some of the things I talked about in families. The longer you put it off, the harder it is to resolve. So ring them up, or go around and say sorry, again! Sometimes it's better to do just that, 'even if you were in the right or wrong'. Just the friendship is all that matters at those moments.

If by these words I have been able to cause reconciliation with someone and their loved ones. It is worth it.

Photo by kind permission Gareth Hughes.

June and Gerald, on their sixty ninth year 2010.

Chapter (20)

A dedication to, Andrew Bryant Griffiths.

Andrew in the hat with his five brothers, Graham, David, Christopher, Gerald, and Peter in the Picture on the wall. When Andrew died on the 2nd October in 2007, I decided I would buy his car from his family estate, so it would be kept in the family. Our Andrew loved his car, and nicknamed it 'Rupert', so Rupert the Rover, 'a Rover 2000'. Some pictures of it, and Andrew, and a picture of my sister Sheila, with his two Children Paul and Zoe.

Angela and Andrew when they were very young at Slimbridge, and Andrew a little older.

Rupert and Andrew & Moe's Dog.   Andrew working on it, and the Interior.

Andrew came home to say his goodbye's. David, Graham, Andrew, Christopher, Gerald. July 2007.

Gerald, Andrew and June about 1999. Moe and Andrew holding Crystal, my sister Sheila's Grandaughter.

Andrew with his car, Rupert the Rover.

Andrew, and sister Angela and her best friend Jean, and Rupert in the background.

Andrew, God bless you, 'Love you mate.'

Chapter (21)

Some of the
Invitations to go to Buckingham Palace.

During my time in leaving the force we have been invited to Buckingham Palace

By

The Queen.

Regarding meeting old comrades and celebrating the 75th years of the formation of

The Grenadier Guards Association.

And

Presentation of new colours to the Regiments on numerous occasions.

On the occasion of the 75th Anniversary
of the formation of the Grenadier Guards Association
The President is commanded by Her Majesty The Queen, Patron
to invite

Mr & Mrs G G Griffiths

to a Garden Party at Buckingham Palace
on Monday 4th July 1988 from 3 pm to 5.30 pm

*The Regimental Lieutenant Colonel, Grenadier Guards
requests the pleasure of the company of*

..........Mr & Mrs G Griffiths..........

*at a Garden Party at Buckingham Palace
on Wednesday 26th July 2000 from 4 - 6pm
by gracious permission of The Queen
and in the presence of
Her Majesty and The Duke of Edinburgh,
to celebrate the 25th Anniversary
of His Royal Highness's appointment as Colonel of the Regiment*

*Dress:
Gentlemen - Lounge suits or Association blazers
Ladies - Day dress, hats optional
Medals*

Admission by ticket only

An Invitation to the Palace Wednesday 26th July 2000.

Buckingham Palace.

Since leaving the Armed Forces, my life has revolved around Martial Arts. I would go to Grenadier Guards Association functions whenever I could, but my Martial Arts and dedication to it was, well, it just happened. Martial Arts came first.

But going to the Gloucestershire Branch of the Grenadier Guards Association was just as important. June and I would always attend their Christmas Draw, as it was a way of raising funds for the Association, which contributed to the welfare of Association Members in need of help for one reason or another. Most of the time, I was able to fit these functions in, or was able to fit them in somehow, and as you can see we enjoyed this very much, really great to see old friends.

'FOR ONCE A GRENADIER ALWAYS A GRENADIER'.

June in Bearskin with members of the Grenadier Guards Band. Pirbright 1987.

This is June and I with Gaz, and was taken

at Pirbright Guards open day 1987.

This is Gaz Gallagher. We were N.C.O.'s working together in the Pioneer Shop at Harding Barracks Wuppertal from 1967 to 1970, then Munster, Germany and England.

This is a picture taken at Pirbright in 1995, when I met my ex Sgt Major Ray Huggins.

Sergeant Major Huggins became my Sgt Major at the end 1967, taking over from Sergeant Major Randle. I remember almost the exact time this happened, as I was on an N.C.O.'s Course. I remember being on the square and was my turn to give commands during drill. Sgt Major Huggins was standing next to me as I shouted my orders. He was helping me along, teaching me the timing and when to shout the commands. Sgt Major Randle was passing down the hill alongside the square to the M.T. Dept, as he was now in charge of the M.T. Section. Looking across, he shouted to Sgt Major Huggins, and quote: 'Give him stick Sgt, Majoooooorr, I want to see what he's like as an N.C.O!' Then walked on.

I was under a lot of pressure as Sgt Major Randle was the one that put my name down for the N.C.O's Course. I think it was Sergeant 'Cloggy' Holmes, from the Pioneer's Shop, where I was now working, that asked Sgt Major Randle to put my name down. By then, I had been a Guardsman for almost five years and Sgt Major Randle thought that was far too long.

This is the same square that the 2nd Grenadier Guards Corps of Drums are marching on, that I done my N.C.O.'s Course in Wuppertal. In the background is the hill that Sgt Major Randle was walking down, which led to the MT and L.A.D. Detachment. Incidentally, my wife June worked for L.A.D. in the offices at that time, as a Clerk on amendments until she had to finish, as she was pregnant with our son, Graham

Grenadier Day Aldershot 2006. First photo, about to go on parade. Second photo, Drum Major Betts talking to: Left Ex-Drum Major Brian Lane RIP, a young Drummer and Ex-Drum Major Peter Nightingale, Coldstream Guards.

Drum Major Betts at the Grenadier Guards Open day in Aldershot 2006.

The open day was amazing, everything was happening.

Not only was there the Guards marching on parade, but there was a great show of talent of wild birds of prey, (Falcons Eagles and Owls). This Eagle flew so high in the sky it was almost out of sight. Some smaller birds started to chase it as it was in there territory, and when it was called back, flew down onto the instructors out held hand, and you could almost see him bare down with the weight of the bird, the wing span being nearly 6 feet across.

There was daring Army Motorbike and Car displays, which was very exciting, going through various flamed obstacles and going over Jumps ECT: There were stalls selling everything from Military items to ice-cream and tea. Not forgetting the Beer tent, where I was able to meet lots of my ex-comrades.

I spent so much time looking and looking to see if I could recognise my old comrades, it was so hard as you are looking and only remember them when they were young, you have to remember that a lot of years has past and we are so much older.

But as I walk around suddenly I hear someone shout hey 'Chinny' which was my army nickname that a Sergeant had given me. I turned around and there was a group of people chatting together, I recognised a couple of men strait away, there was Mick Bullion, and Christopher Beck's, both being in our Platoon as we passed through the Depot at Pirbright at the start of our Army career. There was Sergeant Hughes and other comrades but could not recall all their names, until they introduced their selves. We just chatted for ages all about the old times, it was wonderful.

'A great day to remember'.

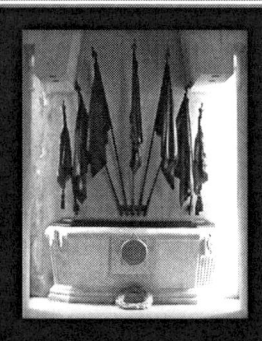

OUT OF THE BLUE A WONDERFUL INVITATION TO GO TO,

THE LAYING UP OF THE OLD COLOURS

OF THE 2ND BATTALION GRENADIER GUARDS, IN BRISTOL CATHEDRAL.

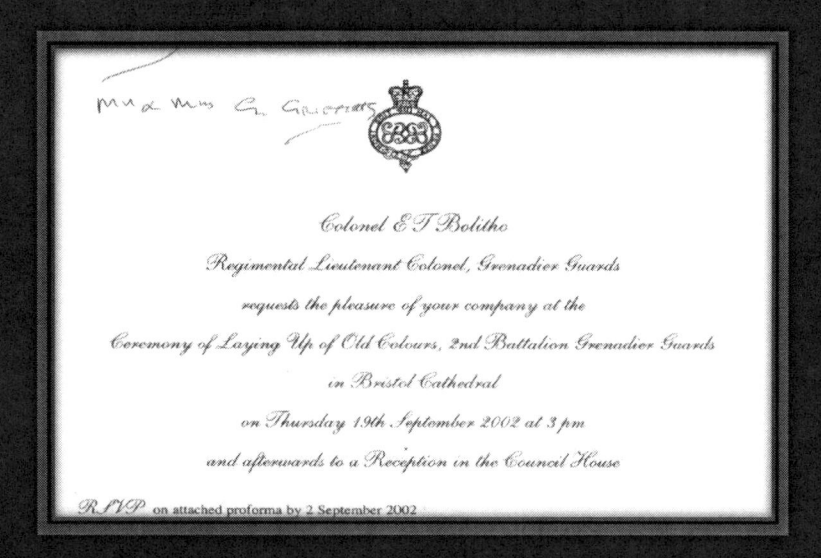

Colonel E T Bolitho
Regimental Lieutenant Colonel, Grenadier Guards
requests the pleasure of your company at the
Ceremony of Laying Up of Old Colours, 2nd Battalion Grenadier Guards
in Bristol Cathedral
on Thursday 19th September 2002 at 3 pm
and afterwards to a Reception in the Council House

RSVP on attached proforma by 2 September 2002

This was a wonderful day, for as you now know I am a Bristol man, born and bred! It was wonderful to see all my old haunts. I managed to meet so many comrades, and some old friends, that I had not seen for such a long time. It just brought back to me the considerable amount of comradeship and friendships that I had made within The Grenadier Guards.

When we are talking and reminiscing about the good and bad old days, the bad times don't seem so bad, and we had a good laugh about them, and thought what Pratt's we sometimes were. But, as I said, the good and the bad times rolled into one, was the overall common factor in the great comradeship that all ex Grenadiers will take through into civilian life, and remain with them until the day they die.

Bristol Cathedral

LAYING UP OF THE
OLD COLOURS OF THE
SECOND BATTALION
GRENADIER GUARDS

Thursday 19 September 2002

3 p.m.

The start of the parade took place at the Queens Square, which is just off Bristol City Centre. Here everyone was getting ready to march to Bristol Cathedral, which is at the bottom of Park Street and next to the City County Council House. We marched out of Queens Square, past the docks on our left and the City Centre on our right, up the hill at the start of Park Street, then along Hotwells Road to the Cathedral on our left.

Hundreds and hundreds of people lined the streets leading to the Cathedral, and as we were marching along, it was like I had gone back in time, and felt as though I was marching down the Mall to Buckingham Palace for the first time all those years ago as a new Guardsman. What with the 50 man Grenadier Guards Band beating the time for our steps, everybody applauded as we swaggered along, and I felt so proud.

The Grenadier Guards Comrades association, preparing to go on parade.

Gerald with Colin Knight, the Secretary of the Gloucestershire Branch of the Grenadier Guards Association. The Gloucestershire Branch has been nominated as the most active Branch in the Association. I personally think this has a lot to do with Mr Colin Knight, and his dedication in the work and contribution he has done for the Branch, plus his contribution with others for the yearly meetings and reunions at Littlecote.

Gerald centre, trying to stand out in the crowd, and ready for the march to the Cathedral.

Television cameras recording Officer's and Gentleman of the parade.

Nearly ready, to form up for the parade.

In the Cathedrel Corp Flute Players.

Grenadier Guards Marching to the Bristol Cathedral.

News cuttings thanks to the evening post Bristol.

BACKGROUND TO TODAY'S SERVICE

The Colours to be laid up today in Bristol Cathedral were presented by Her Majesty The Queen to the 2nd Battalion Grenadier Guards on Horse Guards Parade on 26 May 1992. The Queen's Colour was carried on the Queen's Birthday Parade in 1992 and again in 1994. In August 1994 the 2nd Battalion was placed in suspended animation as part of cuts in the Army. However, the Battalion's customs and traditions are maintained by Nijmegen Company Grenadier Guards. This is an independent Company, currently stationed in Wellington Barracks, with its principal role being Public Duties. All recruits are posted to the Company for a period prior to joining the 1st Battalion.

New Colours were presented by Her Majesty to Nijmegen Company in Buckingham Palace on 15 May 2001 and the Queen's Colour was trooped on the wettest Queen's Birthday Parade in living memory in June last year. The Dean and Chapter of Bristol Cathedral have kindly agreed to accept the old Colours in recognition of the long and close relationship between the Grenadier Guards and the City of Bristol.

Nijmegen Company is so named in honour of the Battle which took place in Holland on 19-21 September 1944 and in which the 2nd Battalion, as part of the Guards Armoured Division played a major part.

ORDER OF SERVICE

Music before the Service:

Sursum Corda	Elgar
Poco allegretto from Symphony No 3	Brahms
Minuet from L'Arlesienne Suite	Bizet
Pomp and Circumstance March No 4	Elgar

The Lord Mayor of Bristol is received at the West Door by the Precentor and is conducted to his place.

Her Majesty's Lord Lieutenant of Bristol is received at the West Door by the Dean and is conducted to his place.

At the entrance of the Choir and Clergy all stand to sing

HYMN

Guide me, O thou great Redeemer,
Pilgrim through this barren land;
I am weak, but thou art mighty;
Hold me with thy powerful hand:
Bread of heaven,
Feed me now and evermore.

Open now the crystal fountain
When the healing stream doth flow;
Let the fiery cloudy pillar
Lead me all my journey through:
Strong deliverer,
Be thou still my strength and shield.

When I tread the verge of Jordan,
Bid my anxious fears subside;
Death of death, and hell's destruction,
Land me safe on Canaan's side:
Songs and praises
I will ever give to thee.

Cwm Rhonnda   *William Williams (1717-1791)*

THE BIDDING
by
Canon Brendan Clover, Precentor of Bristol Cathedral

We have gathered here in the presence of Almighty God and the whole ompany of heaven to offer unto him through our Lord Jesus Christ our worship and praise and thanksgiving; to pray as well for others as for ourselves that we may know more truly the greatness of God's love and show forth in our lives the fruits of his grace; and to ask on behalf of all men such things as their well-being doth require.

It is also our purpose to receive and to lay up in this Cathedral the Old Colours that since 1992 have served as a symbol of the dedication and ideals, comradeship and loyalty, of the Second Battalion Grenadier Guards. As we do so, we offer out thanksgiving to God for his faithfulness to us all, for the service given by the Battalion and by Nijmegen Company to our Queen and Country, and to pray for God's continued protection and blessing upon the life of the Company and the Regiment and their successors in all their future commitments.

All sit

THE ADDRESS
By
The Very Reverend Robert Grimley
Dean of Bristol Cathedral

All remain seated for the Choir to sing

THE ANTHEM

Give Us The Wings of Faith   *Mark Blatchly*

All stand

THE LAYING UP OF THE OLD COLOURS

    Fanfare   Jubilant   *Bliss*

At the approach of the Colours, the Band plays

                Scipio   *Handel*

The Regimental Lieutenant Colonel, having taken his place at the Chancel step, receives the Queen's Colour in his right hand and the Regimental Colour in his left, and turns to face the Altar.

The Precentor says:

Having gathered together in this Cathedral it is our purpose to lay up these Old Colours of the Second Battalion Grenadier Guards. No more fitting place than this house of prayer and praise could be found in which to deposit these emblems of duty and service.

The Regimental Lieutenant Colonel proceeds to the Sanctuary step and says:

These consecrated Colours, formerly carried in the Service of our Sovereign and country, I now deliver into your hands for safe custody within this house of prayer.

The Precentor replies:

I receive these Colours for safe custody within this Cathedral. May all who look upon them be reminded today and in the future of their duty to God, Queen and country; for Jesus Christ's sake. **Amen.**

The Precentor receives the Old Colours and places them upon the Altar.

All remain standing for the Venerable J Blackburn QHC Chaplain General to the Forces, to lead

THE PRAYERS

Let us give thanks to God for the commitment of duty and service, and the exercise of courage and faith, that have been inspired under these Colours; and let us pray for God's blessing on the regimental life of the Grenadier Guards, remembering with particular gratitude all those who have given their lives in its company. With humility and thankfulness we honour their memory and their ready response in the hour of need or conflict.

A short silence follows.

> Lord, hear us.
> **Lord, graciously hear us.**

Let us confess to God ever-merciful the sin, the false pride, the greed and the contempt that mar his image in each human life; and let us pray for his forgiveness: that by the witness of Jesus Christ working in our hearts we may be restored by grace, and remade in the image of his Son.

A short silence follows.

> Lord, hear us.
> **Lord, graciously hear us.**

Let us bring to God our sorrow at the suffering caused by political crisis and armed conflict. Let us offer up prayers for the injured, the disabled and the bereaved, and all who still bear the emotional, spiritual or physical burden of wars long past. We pray that we may never forget their needs, and may readily support the individuals and organizations committed to their care.

A short silence follows.

> Lord, hear us.
> **Lord, graciously hear us.**

As our Saviour commanded and taught us, so we pray:

Our Father, which art in heaven, hallowed be Thy Name. Thy kingdom come, Thy will be done, on earth as it is in heaven. Give us this day our daily bread. And forgive us our trespasses, as we forgive them who trespass against us. And lead us not into temptation, but deliver us from evil: For Thine is the kingdom, the power, and the glory, for ever and ever. **Amen**.

All stand to sing

THE NATIONAL ANTHEM

God save our gracious Queen,
Long live our noble Queen,
God save the Queen.
Send her victorious,
Happy and glorious,
Long to reign over us:
God save the Queen.

Thy choicest gifts in Store
On her be pleased to pour
Long may She reign
May she defend our laws
And ever give us cause
To sing with heart and voice
God Save the Queen

National Anthem   *Author Unknown c1845*

All remain standing for the Reverend Richard Hall, Chaplain to Nijmegen Company to say:

Almighty God, who rulest over all the Kingdoms of the world, we yield thee unfeigned thanks, for that thou hast been pleased to set thy servant our Sovereign Lady Queen Elizabeth, as Colonel-in-Chief of the Grenadier Guards. Let thy wisdom be her guide, and thine arm strengthen her; let truth and justice, peace and charity abound in her days. Direct all her counsels and endeavours to thy glory and the welfare of her subjects; give us grace to obey her cheerfully and let her always possess the hearts of her people; may her reign be long and prosperous, and crown her with everlasting life in the world to come; through Jesus Christ our Lord. **Amen.**

THE REGIMENTAL COLLECT

O God, grant that thy servants the Grenadier Guards may ever be mindful of their proud and costly heritage, that continuing to guard what is right, and fighting for what is just, they may so serve thee here in this life that they may be counted worthy to join those who now continue their service in the life to come; through Jesus Christ our Lord. **Amen.**

All remain standing to sing

HYMN

Praise my Soul, the King of heaven,
To His feet thy tribute bring;
Ransomed, healed, restored, forgiven
Who like thee His praise should sing
Praise Him, praise Him,
Praise Him, praise Him,
Praise the everlasting King.

Praise Him for His grace and favour
To our fathers in distress;
Praise Him, still the same as ever,
Slow to chide and swift to bless:
Praise Him, praise Him,
Praise Him, praise Him,
Glorious in His faithfulness.

Father-like He tends and spares us;
Well our feeble frame He knows;
In His hands He gently bears us,
Rescues us from all our foes:
Praise Him, praise Him,
Praise Him, praise Him,
Widely as His mercy flows.

Angels in the height adore Him;
Ye behold Him face to face;
Sun and moon bow down before Him;
Dwellers all in time and space,
Praise Him, praise Him,
Praise Him, praise Him,
Praise with us the God of grace.

Praise My Soul   *Henry Francis Lyte (1793-1847)*

All kneel. After a short silence the Dean says

THE BLESSING

God give to you and to all those you love,
in this world and the next,
his comfort and his peace,
his light and his joy;
and the blessing of God Almighty,
the Father, the Son and the Holy Spirit
rest upon you and remain with you always. **Amen**

All remain kneeling to sing:

O Trinity of love and power,
Our brethren shield in danger's hour;
From rock and tempest, fire and foe,
Protect them wheresoe'er they go:
Thus evermore shall rise to Thee
Glad hymns of praise from land and sea.

Melita, John Bacchus Dykes (1823-76)   *William Whiting (1825-78)*

All sit. Band and organ play

Crown Imperial   *Walton*

All stand for the Procession to leave the Cathedral.

Gerald and June with a 2nd Battalion Grenadier Guardsman.

A very proud Gerald and June, when they met Gerald's ex Sergeant Major, Mr. Randle and his good lady.

Gerald with 22213678 Ronald Wasley (centre) ex 3rd Bn 1950 -1953 as a Gdsm.

On the left 21006156 Arthur Wareham 3rd Bn 1947-1953 as a L/Sgt,

'Both from Gloucestershire'.

Looking inside this beautiful Bristol Cathedral, note the beautiful stonework.

The Beautiful Stonework of this wonderful Bristol Cathedral.

The 2nd Battalion Grenadier Guards Colours at rest in Bristol Cathedral.

Chapter (22)

This is the Guards Chapel next to Wellington Barracks,

where many of the Guards Colours are at rest.

THE FIRST OR GRENADIER REGIMENT
OF FOOT GUARDS

PRESENTATION OF
NEW COLOURS
TO
THE FIRST BATTALION

by

HER MAJESTY THE QUEEN
Colonel-in-Chief of the Regiment

BUCKINGHAM PALACE
11th May, 2010

Our Wonderful day at Buckingham Palace on the presentation of the New Colours for

The First Battalion Grenadier Guards.

"Tangier, 1680"		"Modder River, 1899"
"Namur, 1695"		"South Africa, 1899-1902"
"Blenheim, 1704"		"Ypres, 1914"
"Gibraltar, 1704-1705"		"Marne, 1914"
"Ramillies, 1706"		"Aisne, 1914"
"Oudenarde, 1708"		"France & Flanders, 1914-1918"
"Malplaquet, 1709"		"Loos, 1915"
"Dettingen, 1743"		"Somme, 1916"
"Lincelles, 1793"		"Cambrai, 1917"
"Egmont-Op-Zee, 1799"		"Arras, 1918"
"Corunna, 1809"		"Hazebrouck, 1918"
"Barrosa, 1811"		"Hindenburg Line, 1918"
"Nive, 1813"		"Dunkirk, 1940"
"Peninsular"		"Mareth, 1943"
"Waterloo, 1815"	"GULF, 1991"	"Monte Camino, 1943"
"Alma, 1854"		"Medjez Plain, 1943"
"Inkerman, 1854"		"Salerno, 1943"
"Sevastopol, 1855"		"Anzio, 1944"
"Tel-El-Kebir, 1882"		"Gothic Line, 1944"
"Eygpt, 1882"		"Nijmegen, 1944"
"Suakin, 1885"		"Mont Pincon, 1944"
"Khartoum, 1898"		"Rhine, 1945"

THE FIRST OR GRENADIER REGIMENT OF FOOT GUARDS

Colonel-in-Chief:
HER MAJESTY THE QUEEN

Colonel:
His Royal Highness The Prince Philip, Duke of Edinburgh KG KT

Regimental Lieutenant Colonel:
Brigadier D J H Maddan

Regimental Adjutant:
Major G V A Baker

Assistant Equerry to His Royal Highness The Prince Philip, Duke of Edinburgh KG KT:
Captain A C T Forster

Assistant Regimental Adjutant:
Captain T A Rolfe

Regimental Quartermaster Sergeant:
WO2 (RQMS) A Hill

ORDER OF CEREMONY

1. The 1st Battalion marches onto Parade, accompanied by the Regimental Band and the Corps of Drums of the Battalion. *(Spectators are to stand and then to be seated when the Battalion halts)*

2. The Regimental Lieutenant Colonel arrives on Parade and is received with a General Salute. The Band plays "Scipio". *(Spectators are to stand)*

3. The Old Colours are marched off Parade to the music of "Auld Lang Syne". *(Spectators are to stand, and then be seated when the Band stops playing)*

4. The Drum Stack is prepared and the new Colours are laid on it. *(Spectators are to remain seated)*

5. The Queen is received on Parade with a Royal Salute. The Band plays the National Anthem. *(Spectators are to stand)*

6. The Queen, accompanied by The Colonel, inspects the Battalion. *(Spectators are to be seated)*

7. The New Colours are consecrated. *(Spectators are to stand)*

8. The Queen presents the New Colours. *(Spectators are to remain standing)*

9. The Queen addresses the Battalion and the Regimental Lieutenant Colonel replies. *(Spectators are to be seated)*

10. The Queen and The Colonel, accompanied by the Regimental Lieutenant Colonel ascend the Terrace steps. *(Officers for the Presentation of Colours rejoin the Battalion and the Drum Stack is removed. Spectators are to remain seated)*

11. The Battalion advances in Review Order and gives a Royal Salute. The Band plays the National Anthem. *(Spectators are to remain seated)*

12. The Battalion gives "Three Cheers" to The Queen.

13. The Queen takes the Salute as the Battalion marches past in threes and marches off Parade. *(Spectators are to stand as the New Colours pass and then resume their seats)*

14. When the Battalion has marched off Parade spectators are to remain in their seats until The Queen has left the Terrace, and then to proceed as swiftly as possible to Wellington Barracks.

THE COLOURS OF THE REGIMENT

The Colours of the Regiment are one of its great glories, and have been carried from its formation until the present day. Over the years military regulations governing Colours have frequently altered. In the Regiment these alterations have been met by the adaptation rather than the cessation of ancient practices; the Colours of the Grenadier Guards today descend directly from the Colours originally granted in 1661, by Royal Warrant of King Charles II, to the Regiments of Lord Wentworth and Colonel Russell.

It may be helpful to have a brief outline of the history of the Colours from the earliest times. It may also avoid misunderstanding if it is made clear that the Company Colours, which have not been on general issue since 1838, should not be confused with the company camp flags which are allotted to Battalions and Companies. The small crimson flags in present use, often incorrectly described as 'company colours', were originally the camp colours used by each Company in camp to mark its lines. Throughout the Army these camp colours normally bore the badge of the Company (that badge borne in the centre of its Company Colour) against a background of the colour of its Regimental facing. In the case of the Regiment, that background became crimson.

It was originally the custom within the Army for every Company to fly its own Colour. When the Regiments of Lord Wentworth and Colonel Russell were incorporated into the Royal Establishments after the restoration of King Charles II, each of the two Regiments was granted twelve Colours by Royal Warrants. On the Colours were painted a selection of the Royal Badges.

The four senior Companies of each of the two Regiments were known as the King's Company, the Colonel's Company, the Lieutenant Colonel's Company and the Major's Company. From the earliest times the Colours of these four senior Companies were distinguished from the remaining Colours, and were known as the Field Officer's Colours. On the amalgamation of Wentworth's and Russell's Regiments in 1665, the Regiment consisted of twenty-four Companies. The four senior Companies of Russell's Regiment became the Sovereign's, Colonel's, Lieutenant Colonel's and Major's Companies, retaining their Colours as before. The Senior Companies of Wentworth's Regiment received new badges, while the sixteen remaining Companies retained their existing ones.

It is from these Senior Company Colours of the Regiment that the Queen's Company Colour and the Queen's Colours of our Battalions today directly descend. The Sovereign's Company Colour, the senior Company Colour of the Regiment, became the Royal Standard of the Regiment. The next three senior – the Standards of the three Field Officers – eventually became the three King's (or Queen's) Colours of Battalions; the Colonel's Company Colour becoming the King's (or Queen's) Colours of the 1st Battalion, the Lieutenant Colonel's that of the 2nd Battalion, and the Senior Major's that of the 3rd Battalion. They are now crimson and not Union; the Queen's Colour of the 1st Battalion carries the Imperial Crown and the 2nd Battalion's (carried by Nijmegen Company) carries the Royal Cypher.

At a certain point in the eighteenth century, the custom of each Company flying its own Colour lapsed, and instead, a Battalion carried one pair or 'stand' of colours, the Sovereign's and Regimental Colours as they are today. Company Colours however continued to exist and to be renewed, and from them the Battalion Colours were chosen.

Queen Victoria's directive of 1859 referred to the 'Company Badges' instead of 'Company Colours', and laid down that these badges should be 'emblazoned in rotation in the centre of the Union or Regimental Colour'. Thus the Company Colour's primary function changed to that of a Battalion Colour. From this time also began the custom of emblazoning the Battalion number in gilt in the sinister canton (the top left hand corner) of the Regimental Colour, instead of the number of the Company to whom the Colour belonged, as had been the case.

COLOURS OF THE 1ST BATTALION
GRENADIER GUARDS

1st Battalion, Grenadier Guards
Queen's Colour

The Queen's Colour is of crimson silk with the Imperial Crown in the centre, a Grenade below, and with the battle honours inscribed. The Grenade was added after the Battle of Waterloo when the change in the Regiment's title, First or Grenadier Regiment of Foot Guards, had been approved, and the custom of inscribing the colours with battle honours dates from 1812 and all Colours have been so inscribed ever since.

1st Battalion, Grenadier Guards

Regimental Colour

The Regimental Colour is the Union Flag, with a company badge in the centre, surmounted by the Imperial Crown and below with the company numeral and the grenade fired proper, with the battle honours inscribed and the number of the Battalion in Roman numerals in the dexter canton. The company badge is XIV Edward IV, "A Falcon with wings expanded argent, beaked legged and belled or within a Fetter Lock closed of the last."

Her Majesty the Queen Presenting the Regimental Colours to the 1st Battalion Grenadier Guards, in the grounds of Buckingham Palace. 11th May 2010.

Photo by kind permission of the Grenadier guards association, the Gloucestershire branch.

Invitation to Buckingham Palace

This was an amazing day, as I met so many of my old comrades, and at one time we were only a few feet away from the Queen, and Prince Phillip.

The Queen looked fantastic, and it was such an honour to be there among such important dignitary's,& Courtesan's of the Palace and of the Grenadier Guards. The colour pomp and ceremony, was fantastic and the Photo's say it all to what a great day it was.

Gerald in front of the stand, where the Queen will sit in a few moments time.

The Worlds press waiting for the Queen to arrive.

The Queen.
Sitting with her Regiment of Foot Guards, the First Battalion Grenadier Guards.

The Queen has had her picture taken with the regiment and is just leaving.

The stand of Guards dismantling after the Queen had departed.

There were Lords and Ladies, and as you can see, Colonels, Majors Captains' and Soldiers of all ranks from Sergeant Majors, Sergeants, down to Guardsman.

June with two of the Officers, Officer on the left carried the
First Battalion Regimental Colours, which was presented by the Queen.

Gerald with two Warrant Officers in the beer tent.

Gerald with one of the Drum Major's.

Mr. Colin Knight, with Drummer Michael. (Junior) and Sergeant Michael Beasley (Senior). This is a rare instance of a father and son serving together at the same time. On the right is Company Sergeant Major Lee Hillier. All three serving Guardsmen are Gloucestershire Branch members.

Gerald with some of his comrades, Left to right: Christopher Beck, (Unknown) Richard Godfrey, Gerald and Chris Harrison.

Left to right: Alice and Alan Holford, Social Secretary for the Gloucestershire branch of the Grenadier Guards association, & John and Yvonne Finch.

Gerald with one of the Sentries in the beer tent.

Outside the beer tent's, you can see the different uniforms of the Drummers and Guardsmen. Second photo: Mr Colin Knight Secutary of the Association Gloucestershire Branch, talking to Sergeant Michael Beasley.

The official photographers of the day. In the Background the public on the edge of Hide-park.

Photo by kind permission, of the Gloucestershire branch of the Grenadier Guards Association.

On a long weekend from the 24th till the 27th of June, we were at The Littlecote Manor for the Grenadier Guards open day. It was a fantastic weekend with so much going on, and got to meet comrades old and new. In the photo we are preparing for the March Past after the blessing for the Regiment and Association Members.

I can be seen to the left of this photo wearing a Guards Beret, and was proud to have been able to wear it that day! The Padre walking by the Drum Head is Eric Davies who did his National Service with the Grenadier Guards. At that time he was not a Clergyman. A really great man and it was a pleasure meeting him on that weekend.

Gerald, with the Town Crier, 'Brian Sylvester'. The Piper is 'Pipe Major Ian King', who was the personal piper to the late Queen Mother. Here he is playing his pipes to the Guest's at the entrance of the Evening-Dinner

Gerald, with his arm around Ex-2nd World War Veteran Ron Hill. The Banner being held of the Grenadier Guards Branch Insignia', by national Serviceman, Ivor Jones. The Gentleman on the left is a 2nd World war Veteran, but it was such a shame as I was not introduced, so cannot recall his name.

Left to right front rank: Jim Hardicre, unknown, unknown, Mick Cotterell, Stan Coombes, Gerald Griffiths, John Gearing and Alan Ford.
Back rank left to right: Roger Gardner, Ian Atherton.

The Grenadier Guards Association
The Windsor, Slough, Branch

I just had to include Roger Dobson, a comrade I often met during many of the Grenadier Guard's open days. Roger and myself were in the same squad during basic training at the Depot, Pirbright.

The top photos show him as he is today, and how he looked on our Squad Photo.

The Wonderful photo on the right is Roger with his Dad 'Major Alan Dobson, M. B. E.' When this photo was taken in 1963, Major Dobson was a Sergeant Major, and a year before this was taken, was the Sergeant Major of the Second Battalion Grenadier Guards at Caterham. He was also my first S/Major. It was after this that S/Major Randle took over from him.

I lost contact with Roger early in my career, and think he may have moved to the 1st Battalion. However, I do recall he was a great person, and someone who could be relied on, which is precisely the kind of comrade you need around you, safe in the knowledge he would be watching your back, as professional Soldiers do in dangerous situations.

Looking at his photo I'm sure his father was rather proud of him, as Roger was no doubt proud of his Dad. Since meeting up with him, I've found that he became Chairman of the Windsor, Slough and District Branch of the Grenadier Guards Association.

Roger was kind enough to allow me to use this photo in my book.

I have been told that the Windsor, Slough Branch has said without Roger's Zeal and Integrity and dedication over the years, the Branch may not have survived.

This reminds me very much of our Gloucestershire Branch secretary Mr Colin Knight, he too has given so much time to the Association. Their time and devotion and dedication to the Grenadier Guards Association Branch's should not go unrecognised. 'We salute you'.

This show's that the Motto of,
Once a Grenadier, always a Grenadier'
will always shines through in everything that an Ex-Grenadier will do.

M y original L/Cpl Stripes, Sniper & Marksman Badges and Signals Insignia.

To/

Her Majesty Queen Elizabeth II
Buckingham Palace,

The Mall London

SW1A 1AA

From/

Mr Gerald Griffiths. The Rea
Bridge House,

Elmore Lane West. Quedgeley.
Gloucester. GL2 3NW

Your Majesty,

Maam, I am an ex-Grenadier Guardsman, and I served nine years in the Grenadier guards, with dedication to Your Majesty and the regiment, from **1961** till **1970**. After coming out of the forces I became a Martial arts Instructor and have been training just over **40** years, since leaving the Grenadier's. I am still a member of the Grenadier Guards Association, within the Gloucester-Shire branch

For all the years in the forces through until this very day, I have kept a journal on some of my experiences in the forces and my Martial arts. Over the last couple of years I have been putting my words into a book form, which is my auto-biography, and all about Martial arts. I hope to get this publish sometime this year.

When I was a child as a baby, during the war years, our house had a direct hit by a German bomb and our house was destroyed. My mother had five children at that time, and we were all put in a home on the Badminton estate, for homeless families, it was called the Queen Mary home at Hinnegar camp, "as I know, you would know", Which was the home of HRH Queen Mary.

I was only six months old when all this happened and I don't have much memory of this. The Queen Mary visited The Camp. She had seen me being held by my Mum and asked to hold me. She said I had a wobbly head. She returned on another visit and asked to see the baby with the wobbly head. Everyone was running around trying to find my Mum to bring me to The Queen. I have a picture of my Mum standing behind the Queen Mary holding me, which is in the pages I have enclosed.

One of the other experiences, I was on Sentry on Winsor Castle, overlooking the long Walk, you came out walking your corgi', "dogs", before you came through the archway one of yours dogs urinated on my boot and, when I came to attention to present arms to your Majesty, it frightened the dog and he was barking at me. You kindly acknowledged my salute and smiled and apologised for your dog. I have put a couple of pictures of where I was on Sentry in Windsor Castle and the Long Walk, in my book

I would like to show you some of the pages, "see enclosed". You could see they are in good taste, and some of the interesting and sad things that has happen in my life, and just recently losing my Mum and a dear sister, "ECT". This is why I decided to put all my memories down into a book form, so my Grandchildren could then show to their Children, in years to come of the interesting stories of my life.

The reason I have written to Your Majesty, these little stories, and the picture of the Long Walk, and HRH Queen Mary and HRH King George V. I would like your kind permission please, to put them in my book. If it is not published, I would still have it made, as I just wanted it for my grandchildren to treasure and pass on to their children, and I would be honoured, if I would be allowed to send Your Majesty a copy whether it is published or not.

I remain Your Majesty's Obedient Servant;   **23862933** L/Cpl Gerald Griffiths. Ex-Grenadiers

signed_____

BUCKINGHAM PALACE

4th May, 2010

Dear Mr. Griffiths,

The Queen has asked me to thank you for your letter of 19th March telling Her Majesty about your nine years' service with the Grenadier Guards, and that in 1970 you left the Regiment to become a Martial Arts instructor.

The Queen was interested to learn that you have been keeping a journal since your years in service and I am to say that it was kind of you to send Her Majesty some pages from the diary.

Careful note has been taken of your request for The Queen's permission to publish your journal. I must tell you, however, that this is not a matter in which Her Majesty would either give or withhold her permission.

I should perhaps mention that the use of pictures of the Royal Family is a matter for the Curator of the Royal Photograph Collection at Windsor Castle who may be able to advise you on the issues of copyright. I am, therefore, forwarding your letter and documentation to that department.

In the meantime, please accept my warm good wishes.

Yours sincerely,

Mrs. Sonia Bonici
Senior Correspondence Officer

Gerald Griffiths, Esq.

A letter from the Queen.

22, FRIARY COURT,
ST. JAMES'S PALACE,
LONDON. SW1A 1BQ

17th January, 1981

Dear Mr. Griffiths,

Princess Alexandra has asked me to thank you very much for your letter.

The Princess is greatly touched by the kind invitation that you have conveyed on behalf of Quedgeley Karate Club for her to come to the Disco and Buffet on the occasion of the Students of the Year awards and it is, therefore, with the utmost regret that she has to let you know she is unable to accept.

Needless to say, as Patron of the National Kidney Research Fund, Her Royal Highness is extremely grateful to hear that the members of the Club are raising funds for kidney research and she would so like to have been in a position to join with you all for the evening. However, the programme for the next few months has already been settled and, although she has had another careful look at her diary, the Princess unfortunately finds that she simply cannot manage to fit in a visit to Gloucestershire on Friday, the 13th February.

Princess Alexandra is nevertheless so sorry to have to give a disappointing answer and she only hopes you will understand her predicament. In thanking you for asking her, the Princess also hopes that the Awards evening will prove to be a most successful and enjoyable event for the Club and, to you and your members, she sends her warmest good wishes.

In case it is helpful, I would mention that I am forwarding a copy of your letter to the Director of the National Kidney Research Fund, Mr. W. P. Mullen, and I am sure he could arrange something if you would like the Fund to be represented on the 13th February.

Yours sincerely,

Mona Mitchell
Private Secretary

Gerald Griffiths Esq.

A letter from Princes Alexandra.

10th September 2000

Dear Gerald,

Please excuse the typing rather than a hand-written letter, but you probably would'nt be able to read it!

I was delighted to receive the other day an enormous envelope containing your life-history! It was so kind of you to think of sending it all and I was fascinated to see what you have been doing all these years. Of course, I did have an idea from previous meetings with you and from what you have told me, but to see it all well documented was quite a different thing and I have much enjoyed reading it all. I am not sure the Slendertone pictures are'nt a bit of a con! You are clearly adopting a very different pose, but I am sure that those who do'nt know you would be totally taken in!

You have achieved a great deal in life and can be justifiably proud of yourself. What I like is that so much has been done for others rather than just for yourself, but then I always knew that that was very much a part of your character. You have done so well with your martial arts and, though it has never been something that has interested me personally, I can see the attraction and usefulness of it, and it is wonderful that there are people like yourself who give freely of their time to help others in this way.

The military photographs all brought back happy memories of a wonderful era in my life and it was people like yourself who helped to make it the fun that it was. I remember that photograph being taken in Amsterdam, funnily enough! It is extraordinary what one remembers!

I am most impressed by the singing, and even more by the composing! You are kind to have sent me a CD and I shall enjoy listening to it. Shall I play it at the next Branch meeting to show the members what talent there is amongst Association members?!

I am about to end another era in my life, as I am pulling out of farming. You will have read in the Press how bad it is at present and they are not exaggerating. I am selling everything except the land, which I am going to let out to someone else to have a go, and good luck to them! It is not easy. I suppose it is about time I retired. I have been doing it since 1970 and it is now the moment to give time to one or two other things.

It was very good to have seen you both at Buckingham Palace and what a splendid party it was. Made one feel proud to be British and to have been a Grenadier! Keep in touch and good luck with all you are doing.

Very best wishes from us both to you and Tune,
Yours sincerely, Hamish Gray-Cheape

A kind letter from an officer, Captain H. L. Gray'Cheape, I worked for as a driver of a Ferret Scout Car.

God and the soldier,
we alike adore

In times of danger,
not before.

The danger past
and all conflict righted,

God is forgotten,
the soldier slighted.

THE FINAL INSPECTION

The soldier stood and faced God,
Which must always come to pass.
He hoped his shoes were shining,
just as brightly as his brass.

'Step forward now, you soldier,
how shall I deal with you?
Have you always turned the other cheek?
To My Church have you been true?'

The soldier squared his shoulders and said,
'No, Lord, I guess I ain't.
Because those of us who carry guns,
Can't always be saint's.

I've had to work most Sundays,
and at times my talk was tough.
And sometimes I've been violent,
because the world is awfully rough.

But, I never took a penny,
that wasn't mine to keep...
Though I worked a lot of overtime,
when the bills got just too steep.

And I never passed a cry for help,
though at times I shook with fear.
And sometimes, God, forgive me,
I've wept unmanly tears.

I know I don't deserve a place,
among the people here.
They never wanted me around,
except to calm their fears....

If you've a place for me here, Lord,
It needn't be so grand.
I never expected or had too much,
but if you don't, I'll understand...

There was a silence all around the throne,
where the saints had often trod.

As the soldier waited quietly,
for the judgement of his God.

'Step forward now, you soldier,
you've borne your burdens well...
Walk peacefully on Heaven's streets,
you've done your time in Hell.'

Author Unknown~

Hi Gerald,

I hope all is well. I thought I'd send you a rough draft of your story for Emigrate Australia, so you can check the information is correct. Feel free to let me know if there is anything you're not happy about. Also, will you be able to send me a picture for use alongside the article?

Regards,

David

It may have taken him a little longer than the rest of his family to decide that Australia is where his future lay, but 66-year-old Gerald Griffiths is determined to prove that when it comes to immigrating to Australia, age is no barrier.

"I already have one brother and two sisters out in Australia at the moment, while my son and grandchildren also live out there," says Gerald. "I did have two brothers out there at one point, but one has sadly passed away."

Having relatives living in different parts of Australia – his brother and one of his sisters live in Sydney, the other sister resides in Adelaide while his son is in Brisbane – means that Gerald, who has visited the country on five previous occasions, has seen various parts of Oz over the years, but it is Brisbane where he is intending to settle, close to his son and grandchildren.

So what has suddenly prompted him to make the move Down Under? "My wife, June, and I have now retired from our day jobs, and it just feels like the right thing for us to do," he answers.

While emigrating will mean the Griffiths' will have to sell their treasured house beside the Rea Bridge in Gloucester – a gift from the Waterways for whom Gerald worked as a Bridge man for 23 years up until the age of 50 – the couple are really excited about starting the next chapter of their life. "We are getting on in years, but we're not too old to make this great decision," he says.

The couple are currently going through the process of obtaining a Parent visa, with their son, obviously, as the sponsor, and a nephew – one of Gerald's sister's sons – acting as the assuror of support.

"We considered going through the process alone as it should be quite straightforward," explains Gerald. "But in the end we decided to use a migration agent as it would be a lot easier and take the pressure off us.

"Our agent came recommended by a director of GR Lanes Health Products, a company I used to work for, who emigrated a couple of years ago. I figured that he was a businessman who knew what he was talking about so this would be a good enough recommendation."

So, has he been happy with the level of support he has received to date?
"I've found the agents very helpful," Gerald responds. "To be honest I haven't really had to do anything. It's just been a case of sign here, sign there and let them get on with it. We've even been provided with a list of recommendations by the agency for other companies we could consider using for other stages of the process, such as removals.

"The only frustrating thing about the whole process really is the waiting".
Gerald and June hope to be out in Australia by the end of next summer, and are counting down the days.
However, while at 66 years of age you could forgive Gerald for simply wanting to put his feet up and enjoy his retirement amid his new, warmer surroundings, nothing could be further from the truth.

"I'm planning to open up my own martial arts dojo out there," explains Gerald, who has been practising martial arts, mostly karate and tai chi along with various weapon-based disciplines, for over 40 years. He is currently the chief instructor for Shotos Traditional Karate Ka – practising Shoto-Kai and Shoto-Kai forms of karate – in Gloucester (www.shotostkk.com).

"I've been interested in martial arts ever since my days in the Grenadier Guards many years ago," he tells me. "I was in the armed forces for nine years during which time I became very keen on unarmed combat, learning how to disarm people carrying knives and so on."

It's even possible that Gerald's interest in martial arts during his time in the forces rubbed off on a future monarch.
"In 1962 the late King Hussein of Jordan and I were on manoeuvres together," recalls Gerald. "He was impressed with some of my knife throwing and how I could make them stick in trees from distance and asked me how I did it.

"A few years later I saw in one of the combat magazines I buy that he had achieved a black belt in karate. I like to think I contributed to this in some way," he adds with a laugh.

As yet Gerald admits that he hasn't really looked into possible locations for his Brisbane-based dojo, and that he is waiting until they arrive in Australia before he starts to look. He has, however, been thinking about what it will look like.

"There's a gym under JJB Sports in Gloucester that's very impressive," he says. "I've taken a few photos of it to give me some ideas."

Not that Gerald is planning on making a living from the dojo. "It'll be used for a hobby rather than a business," he explains. "I'm probably a bit too old to be getting involved in all the bits and pieces you need to operate a business, so it's just something for me, and a few friends to use.

"Of course, if it starts to take off I'll consider starting it as a business, but... well, we'll see."
For now, though, Gerald and June only have their sights on getting the visas that will enable them to join the various other members of their family in Oz.

"Our life will be just starting," states Gerald. "We are just so excited about it."

Chapter (23)

I am sitting here, we have just seen the New Year in and it is now the second of January 2011. I am reminiscing over the last six or seven months, and thinking how exciting this last year has been, and what a year it has been! We have sold our beautiful Rea Bridge House on the Canal, and purchased a Bungalow in Dursely, 'so we're still in Gloucestershire'.

As we could not move in for three weeks, we had to live in a hotel, so went on Holiday to Butlins in Somerset, and managed to move in on our return on the 7th of June. We had no furniture apart from a bed, two chairs and a table, as all our belongings were in the process of being shipped to Australia, yes, Australia! We lived in the Bungalow for a month while waiting to move, and during that month, time seemed to pass quickly. It was an exciting time, and managed to squeeze in a trip to the Grenadier Reunion at Littlecote, as well as attend the Queen's Presentation of New Colours to the 1st Battalion Grenadier Guards, at Buckingham Palace.
These are the wonderful colour photo's you've just seen, of which only a fraction are shown.

We have now moved Down-Under and arrived in Australia on the 2nd of July 2010, where Angela's son Paul and wife Cheryl were kind enough to put us up at their home in Seaford South Australia. I cannot convey enough gratitude for their generosity in allowing us to stay with them. Thank you Paul and Cheryl so much. We then moved into rented accommodation the fifteenth of July. I am sitting here writing, thinking of all those wonderful things. It is now 2nd January and today we have been here six months! I am rather warm, as this is their wonderful summer.

Angela's son Paul, with his wife, Cheryl and their children, Morgan and Will.

This Photo I am Showing my father's Medals which has to be worn on the right side of the chest, which I carry with so much pride, are my Father's Medals, from when Dad served in the British Royal Navy protecting the fleets of Convoys in the cold Atlantic Waters of Russia, during the 2nd World War.

This is a Artilary Gun outside the R.S.L. Which is quite a landmark in Port Noarlunga.

Gerald wore his Medals for the Anzac early morning dawn service at the R.S.L. in Port-Noarlunga, Christy's Beach, South Australia, on the 25th April 2011. This was his first Parade in Australia, which was to show his respect for all fallen Soldiers throughout the World.

This parade was so well attended and in Australia it is become quite a well-known fact that a lot more of the younger generation are showing interest, and respect for this parade. My wife June and my Nephews wife Cheryl came to the parade, Cheryl said she was very proud to stand next to me, on Parade.

They shall not grow old,

as we that are left grow old.

Age shall not weary them, nor the years condemn.

At the going down of the sun and in the morning,

We shall remember them.

My Dad's Meals

Left to right: 1939-45 Star, Atlantic Star with France and Germany Clasp, Defence Medal, War Medal, Arctic Campaign Commemorative Medal, Russian Convoy medal.

On Christmas Day we went down onto the beach and along the esplanade for a beautiful walk, we also went for a drive in our lovely Morris Minor that we had exported to Australia with us. Even as I write, England is in a big freeze and the weather is bad, so I think we have done the right thing by coming down here, we hope?

We are now house hunting, Oh! By the way, we have rented the bungalow out in England, as a backup in case we change our minds, but I don't think we will, especially after seeing the pictures of the bad snow they are having back home.

I think I had better close my writings for now, otherwise this journal will go on forever, all that remains now is to put in a few beautiful photos of our house, that we will miss, and some of our family members photos that I have missed out, as keepsakes for them all to show that I have not forgotten them. If I have forgotten anyone, its ether I did not have a decent photo of them, or you know I am human and mistakes can happen, BUT I LOVE YOU ALL!

June and Gerald, down on the beach with Moggy in Australia, winter 2010.

This is a picture I took at the Hempstead Bridge, not far from the Rea Bridge.

These two photos taken on Rea Bridge, looking down the Canal.

I took these two photos from a Cherry Picker that changes the street lighting.
The Soren Larsen from the Television Series the Onedin Line.

This is what we saw every day outside our old home; they came to our gate to feed.

Gerald, with his three brothers, Graham, David and Christopher.

This is a Picture of June about ten years old, with Christopher and Tony with their Mum.

Janice and Ray's wedding. Gerald, Chris, June, the Bride & Groom, Mama Parker, Diane & Tony

June's Brothers and Sister.
Left to right: Gerald, Christopher, June Janis, Tony and Janis's Daughter, Karen.

June and her two nieces, Shula and Karen. June with her Mum and sister Janis and Janis's two children, Karen and Shula.

Glenis & Graham a lovely picture of my Mum, Gran Griffiths, Mark and his family.
Tina and there lovely baby Charlotte. Then Tracy, Shaun's Wife, with Debby's daughter Kayleigh.

Leon Gleadall & Kayleigh, and Lauren with their Mum, Debby, Hayley" Graham's daughter's & Jack.

Graham and Glenis with their son Brett.   Brett and Sally.

David, Sheila, Janet, Mary and Julie.

Keith and Sheila.

Annette, Julie and Tracy.

Annette, Julie and Tracy.

Penny (Janet) and Christopher.

Christopher, David, Mum, Gerald, Graham at back.

Gerald and June.

June's Mum and Dad.

Age is no barrier for martial arts enthusiast

It may have taken him a little longer than the rest of his family to decide that Australia is where his future lay, but 66-year-old Gerald Griffiths is determined to prove that when it comes to emigrating to Australia, age is no barrier, writes **David Fuller**.

"I already have one brother and two sisters out in Australia at the moment, while my son and grandchildren also live out there," says Gerald. "I did have two brothers out there at one point, but one has sadly passed away."

Having relatives living in different parts of Australia – his brother and one of his sisters live in Sydney, the other sister resides in Adelaide while his son is in Brisbane – means that Gerald, who has visited the country on five previous occasions, has seen various parts of Oz over the years, but it is Brisbane where he is intending to settle, close to his son and grandchildren.

So what has suddenly prompted him to make the move Down Under? "My wife, June, and I have now retired from our day jobs, and it just feels like the right thing for us to do," he answers.

While emigrating will mean the Griffiths' will have to sell their treasured house beside the Rea Bridge in Gloucester – a gift from the Waterways for whom Gerald worked as a bridgeman for 23 years up until the age of 50 – the couple are really excited about starting the next chapter of their life. "We are getting on in years, but we're not too old to make this great decision," he says.

The couple are currently going through the process of obtaining a Parent visa, with their son, obviously, as the sponsor, and a nephew – one of Gerald's sister's sons – acting as the assurer of support.

"We considered going through the process alone as it should be quite straightforward," explains Gerald. "But in the end we decided to use a migration agent as it would be a lot easier and take the pressure off us.

"Our agent came recommended by a director of GR Lanes Health Products, a company I used to work for, who emigrated a couple of years ago. I figured that he was a businessman who knew what he was talking about so this would be a good enough recommendation."

So, has he been happy with the level of support he has received to date?

"I've found the agents very helpful," Gerald responds. "To be honest, I haven't really had to do anything. It's just been a case of sign here, sign there and let them get on with it. We've even been provided with a list of recommendations by the agency for other companies we could consider using for other stages of the process, such as removals.

"The only frustrating thing about the whole process really is the waiting."

Gerald and June hope to be out in Australia by the end of next summer, and are counting down the days.

However, while at 66 years of age you could forgive Gerald for simply wanting to put his feet up and enjoy his retirement amid his new, warmer surroundings, nothing could be further from the truth.

"I'm planning to open up my own martial arts dojo out there," explains Gerald, who has been practising martial arts, mostly karate and tai chi along with various weapon-based disciplines, for over 40 years. He is currently the chief instructor for Shotos Traditional Karate Kai – practising Shoto-Kan and Shoto-Kai forms of karate – in Gloucester (www.shotostkk.com).

"I've been interested in martial arts ever since my days in the Grenadier Guards many years ago," he tells me. "I was in the armed forces for nine years during which time I became very keen on unarmed combat, learning how to disarm people carrying knives and so on."

It's even possible that Gerald's interest in martial arts during his time in the forces rubbed off on a future monarch.

"In 1962 the late King Hussein of Jordan and I were on manoeuvres together," recalls Gerald. "He was impressed with some of my knife throwing and how I could make them stick in trees from distance and asked me how I did it.

"A few years later I saw in one of the combat magazines I buy that he had achieved a black belt in karate. I like to think I contributed to this in some way," he adds with a laugh.

As yet Gerald admits that he hasn't really looked into possible locations for his Brisbane-based dojo, and that he is waiting until they arrive in Australia before he starts to look. He has, however, been thinking about what it will look like.

"There's a gym under JJB Sports in Gloucester that's very impressive," he says. "I've taken a few photos of it to give me some ideas."

Not that Gerald is planning on making a living from the dojo. "It'll be used for a hobby rather than a business," he explains. "I'm probably a bit too old to be getting involved in all the bits and pieces you need to operate a business, so it's just something for me, and a few friends to use.

"Of course, if it starts to take off I'll consider starting it as a business, but… well, we'll see."

For now, though, Gerald and June only have their sights on getting the visas that will enable them to join the various other members of their family in Oz.

"Our life will be just starting," states Gerald. "We are just so excited about it."

■ Gerald and June Griffiths are using Ian Harrop and Associates to aid them with the emigration process.www.ianharrop.co.uk

Martial arts fanatic Gerald Griffiths is excited about starting his new life Down Under

Chapter (24) THE BIBLIOGRAPGHY & INDEX

Military and press cuttings, and photos, with kind permission to.

Thanks to the Dursley Gazette, for press cutting of: a special Mum. ----------Page 10.

Poem of, Angels on earth, by Kathleen Shields, 14th May 2006. ----------Page12.

Letter from Jane Cook, eulogy of my Mum. ----------Page 13.

The HMS, Bramble, HMS Hood off the internet. Wikipedia, the free encyclopaedia ----------Page's 32 to 33.

The HMS Ark Royal and Photo of Mr Adris Rubin White, thanks to his son, Erick and his wife Jenny White, for contributing these photo. ----------Page 35.

A press cutting from years ago, that our family had kept, showing Queen Mary taken at Hinnagar Camp on the Badminton Estate, about February 1942. (Unknown paper). ---------- Page 38.

A photo of the Bristol Docks basin, overlooking Clifton. ----------Page 43.

The information on the flowers and Clifton Suspension Bridge, from Wikipedia, the free encyclopaedia. ----------Page 54.

Photos Rifles and weapons ----------Page 75.

Grenadier Bugler, kind regards from Barry ----------Page 87.

Bugler, London GB.Com ----------Page 88.

Photos of Kaiteur Falls, an aerial shot of Georgetown, (Guyana web site) Guyana news and information www.guyana.org ---------- Pages 100 to 103.

Snakes, Anaconda, Rattle Snakes, Alligator, and Owl. {Guyana web site} www. Guyana.org -------- Pages 105, 106,109,110.

Pirbright Assault Course unknown. ----------Page 113.

Picture and information of King Hussein of Jordon, from their Web site. ----------Page 114.

Windsor Castle and the Long Walk. Royal House of Windsor. ----------Pages, 116, 117, 119.

Ferret Fox Scout Car, Unknown. ----------Page 147.

I would like to acknowledge and thank David Higgs for allowing me to use----------Pages 144, 146, 147, 149.

A Sennelarger Landscape, from the Wikipedia, the free encyclopaedia. ---------- Page 148.

I would like to acknowledge thank Richard Thomas Godfrey, for his photos ----------Page 150, 151.

Photos of the Armoured Personal Carriers, FV 432, and the FV 603 Saracen. ----------Pages 150, 151.

Bibliography and Index continued.

A photo of Paderborn Barracks, that is from the Wikipedia, the free encyclopaedia. --------------------Page 152.

I would like to acknowledge and thank Gaz Gallagher for the photo. ---------------------------------------Page 154.

Photo of Trooping the Colour in the Mall. London GB.com ---Page 155.

Officers on the Square at Chelsea Barracks, Captain Gray 'Cheap & the Master of Rollo. Russell Braddon.

All the Queens men. I have written to them on numerous occasions with no reply.   -------------------Page 155.

Photo of Tower of London & a Beefeater. London GB.com. ---Page 158.

Pamphlet of the Presentation of the 2nd Battalions Grenadier Guards Colours. --------------------------Page 160.

The information and photo of Sir Harold Alexander. From the Wikipedia, the free encyclopaedia. -Page 157.

Shadows star livens up party. Thanks to the Gloucester Citizen. --Page 182.

Bristol Cathedral pamphlet on the laying up of the 2nd Grenadier Guards Colours. --- Pages 242, 246, to 250.

Three press cuttings from the Evening Post, on the Laying up of the 2nd Btn Grenadier Guards .Page 245, 246.

The, 1st Battalion Grenadier Guards, pamphlet on ceremony of New Colours. ----------------- Pages 257, to 262.

Buckingham Palaces invite. --- Page 263.

A photo of Trooping the New Colours. London GB.com. -- Page 270.

A wonderful letter from the Queen. Thank you. --Page 271.

A wonderful letter from Princess Alexandra. Thank you. -- Page 272.

A wonderful letter from Captain Gray 'Cheap. Thank you --Page 273.

A poem that I had in an Email, The final inspection. ---Page 274.

Thanks to Mr. Colin Knight for his email allowing the photos from the Grenadier Guards Association Gloucestershire branch, for my book. www.gloucestershiregrenadiers.co.uk ; Pages 274 and bottom picture page 281.

Thu, 27 January, 2011 2:28:03 Re: Feedback Form: Permission for photos Amral Khan <amralkhan@rogers.com> Add to Contacts From To griffoneofnine@yahoo.co.uk Hello
Yes you can go ahead and use the pictures, Please be sure to give credit to the website for the use of the picture.
Good luck Regards
Amral Khan
Administrator
EmailMeForm wrote: Your Name*: Gerald Griffiths Your Email Address*:griffoneofnine@yahoo.co.uk Subject*: Permission for photos Message*:Dear sir, I served in the British armed force The Grenadier Guards in Guyana in 1963-64 and I am writing my Biography of my life and of the time, when I was in Guyanaon a peace keeping force. There is a chapter on the time I served in your wonderful country and I would like your kind permission to put some photos of Kaieteur waterfalls in my book as when I visited there. And a photo of George Town from the Air. I have only talked very highly of your beautiful country and My story goes right back to when I was a child and is all about my memories I look forward to an early reply. Kind regards Gerald Glyn Griffiths where are you viewing us from*: I am British and have just moved to Australia to live

Natalie Amy Paternoster01 February 2011 at 22:02
Re: hi'ya i served with your dad.
Wow - Hello!!!!
Thank you for your e mail and yes you are more than welcome to use the photograph's you requested!! I do all I can to keep my dear dad s memory alive x Natalie. This is Mrs Shellys Daughter, Dick Shells Wife. Thank for Photos pages; 161, and 162.

Stuart Davis February 6 at 7:40pm Report

This is my second try Gerald.
Use the picture by all means no worries. It was taken in the Gulf circa 68/69 when I was a young L/Cpl.
the gun is a Mobat 120mm recoilless as you will remember. I was lucky enough to use all three guns that came into service. Mobat, Wombat (which was vehicle mounted) and the Conbat which was a converted Mobat. Instead of the Bren spotter it was fitted with a 0.5 mm spotting rifle. This had a similar trajectory as the main armament unlike the Bren. So it was a hit with the spotter and "standby". A similar weapon was also mounted on the Wombat. Being with the 2nd Bn's A/T at the time you were, can you remember a chap named Brian Withers? He was in the Para Coy for a while but he was also with the 2nd Bn's A/T.
Best regards Stu. Davis if you have got this twice I apologise but I'm crap with this face-book.

Gerald Griffiths February 7 at 12:27am

Thank you Stuart that is fantastic it will make my little story about the Mobat and Wombat gun much more exciting, having someone standing behind it. Page, 96.

From: Gerald Griffith

To: grenadiersglos@tiscali.co.uk

Sent: Wednesday, February 16, 2011 12:41 AM

Subject: Trying again as thought last one had not gone

Dearest Colin,

Just sending this again as I think it may not have got sent the last time. Sorry if you did get it, as I don't wish to be a nuisance.

So, so, close to finishing my book. I was wondering if I can have your kind permission to put these pictures in from the Grenadier guards Association website, one is at Little-cot as I am in the picture at the back, and of the Queen presenting the Colours, I have put them on here so you can see which ones, If you cannot, don't feel bad I understand. I am so pleased how my book has gone even to where the Guyana government of where I served has given permission of photos of Kaieteur falls in Guyana, and a Captain that I was Scout Car driver to Captain Gray 'Cheap has given me a photo of himself in full guard order. I will send you the CD soon.
We are going on fine out here and settling down still have not bought our own place yet. Kind regards Love Gerald & June. When do you want to come down? You are most welcome. Hope you and your family are keeping well.
Very Kind regards Love Gerald & June

From: Colin Knight <grenadiersgloucestershire.co.uk>

To: Gerald Griffiths <griffoneofnine@yahoo.co.uk>

Dear Gerald. No. I have not had this e-mail before there is no problem using the picture from

Littlecote. As I understand it pictures taken from the association website there is no

Problem in reproducing them as long as they do not bring the regiment into disrepute

Which of course they will not in your book.

Trust that you and June are well. Australia is certainly hitting the world news with the

Weather problems that you have been having. I do hope that you have not been affected in anyway.

Captain Gray Cheap is president of the Worcester Branch. I have met up with him

Several times now. Seems a very decent sort of chap. Regards, Colin.

Hello Gerald.
I didn't realise you'd sent the part with the photo's in another e-mail and have only just found them.

A couple of tweaks needed here I'm afraid, <u>Which I've done for you in this reply</u>, which I hope you approve? and Oh! I wasn't the tallest Corps member, Big Ken Smith was 6 foot 7 and towered above me! (but you can leave that in if you wish)
You know you're more than welcome to use anything you like, no need to ask as I won't be suing you for breach of copyright once you've made a fortune with your book.
If you remember I spoke to Natalie and she said she's pleased you're using her dad's photo's as it's helping keep his memory alive, which she's been trying to do, so no problems there.
From Richard Lee Nettleton.

Dear Mr Griffiths

Thank you for your email which has been passed on to Permissions. I am afraid that I have been unable to trace the original contract or any other rights information regarding the above title. I cannot, therefore, give you formal permission to use pictures from this book.

Whilst Penguin has no objection to the use of the pictures, we cannot warrant that such use would not infringe any third party rights, and it must be at your own risk should you wish to proceed. Please include details of the original publication and a disclaimer in your list of acknowledgements. I apologise for being unable to help further in this matter. Best wishes Hayley

Hayley Davidson

Permissions Assistant
Penguin Books Ltd, 80 Strand, London WCR 0RL
Fax: +44 (0) 20 7010 67

From: gerald griffiths [mailto:griffoneofnine@yahoo.co.uk]
Sent: 16 May 2011 08:04
To: Hamish Hamilton (PUK)
Subject: Copy Rights. Dear Sir or Madam, I am at present writing my Autobiography, I am an ex Grenadier Guardsmen, and served twelve years in the 2nd Battalion Grenadier guards and was a Batman and Ferret Scout Car driver to an Officer named Captain Gray'Cheap, we were stationed In Germany together but was also stationed at Chelsea Barracks. During this time Russell Braddon had written a Book called, (All the Queens Men). Of which I have one in my possession. In this Book there is a picture of my Captain Gray'Cheap, on Page 159 of the Book, which is the only Photo on that page': The Officer in question is on the right. I am hoping for your kind permission to enclose this Photo in my Autobiography which is conducive to the fact I was working with him. Of course putting the Credits to Russell Braddon, (All the Queens Men) and your, publishing company.   I look forward to your early reply.   Very kind regards. Yours sincerely. Gerald Glyn Griffiths.

This email was sent by a company owned by Pearson plc, registered office at 80 Strand, London WC2R 0RL.
Registered in England and Wales with company number 53723

Tue, 17 May, 2011 14:23:15
Roger Dobson posted on your Wall.
From Facebook fbmessage+zegoqrr1@facebookmail.com>
Add to Contacts
To: Gerald Griffiths <griffoneofnine@yahoo.co.uk>

Roger Dobson posted on your Wall. Reply to this email to comment on this post.

Roger Dobson

Hi Chinny, you may of course use the photo of me and the old man it goes without saying. Roger about an hour ago
·LikeUnlike·

I sincerely hope you have enjoyed reading about my Life and time's in the

2nd Battalion Grenadier Guards.

There is another book on the Martial Arts

Shoto's Traditional Karate Kai.

On Health, Safety and Diet.

And mainly on the best ideals on teaching methods of my experience that I have been able to obtain first hand, from

Years of teaching.